Endorsements

This book provides va... playing the fruit of the Spirit, such as gentleness and patience. Pastor Ruth provides us with such timely and relatable illustrations taken from life's journey, which we can all appreciate. The book speaks to these virtues with a clarity that will help us develop and maintain relationships and open doors for us to reach out to others.

—Rev. Carson Atherley
Senior Staff, IS/IVCF, Barbados

Instructive, experiential, and engaging. This devotional draws us to Paul's instructions in Galatians 5 on the importance of cultivating the fruit of the Holy Spirit in our lives. It points to the need to yield to the Spirit of Christ, allowing His power, His fruit, and His gifts to be demonstrated in our lives. Understanding the strength provided through gentleness and self-control helps in focusing on Him in the challenges we face. Thank you, Ruth, for the reminders that Christ is our everything!

—Patricia Allison
Intercessor, Presbyterian Reformed Ministries International
Dunamis Fellowship Canada

Ruth Teakle's book on gentleness and self-control truly depicts the heart of our Saviour. Jesus lived and walked with a spirit of gentleness, and He desires for us to do the same. Every day Ruth gives us an easy-to-swallow "truth nugget" to live out. Thank you, Ruth, for this spiritually challenging book. A must-read for every Christian.

—Steven Stoffelsen
Author of *Trusting God's Timing*
Founder of House of Refuge Street Ministries
www.houseofrefuge.ca

This devotional couldn't have come at a better time! Ruth Teakle invites us to the table with a delightful thirty-day feast on the fruit of the Spirit, loaded with the extravagant special flavours of gentleness and self-control. Her wealth of real-life experiences in her life journey with her family, ministry, and her deep walk with the Lord are intricately woven together with such a breath of freshness and reality of truth. Her heart of compassion and intimacy with God invites us to savour the joy and peace that emerge from practising a gentle spirit, enjoying forgiveness, and relishing a life not governed by strife. At a time when we are being ravaged by a dangerous rise in hardened hearts and self-centred, intolerant attitudes that hurt others, this devotional opens the door to healthy relationships and a life of shalom in Christ Jesus.

—Pastor Amenla Cunningham
Women's Pastor, First AG Church, Bangalore, India
www.firstagchurch.in

I was introduced to Ruth's powerful and encouraging writing through *Pursuing Peace*, and this new volume, *Gentleness and Self-Control*, does not disappoint. Relatable, scriptural, and practical. Whether you read this gem over thirty days or savour it and go more slowly, be prepared to be uplifted and challenged in your walk with the Lord. Truly timely and timeless.

—Vivian Bright
Training Facilitator, Caring for the Wounded Heart
School Principal, Ottawa area
www.connectingstreams.com

"I wonder what our desperate world would look like if we entrusted ourselves to the One who knows us best" (Ruth Teakle). My long-time friend and colleague will gently lead you into your Heavenly Father's "heart of love," where you will learn to "cultivate and reap" a rich harvest of patience, peace, kindness, goodness, gentleness, and self-control in your life.

—Sandra E. Noel RN (retired)
Former Provincial Prayer Coordinator, Women's Ministries PAONL
Former National Board Member, Women's Aglow Canada
Present Member, International Committee
International Friendship League, iflworld.org

Cultivating Gentleness & Self-Control

A 30 Day Devotional Journey

Cultivating Gentleness & Self-Control

A 30 Day Devotional Journey

Ruth Teakle
& a Company of Friends

CULTIVATING GENTLENESS AND SELF-CONTROL
Copyright © 2023 by Ruth Teakle

All rights reserved. Neither this publication nor any part of this publication may be reproduced or transmitted in any form or by any means, electronic or mechanical, including photocopying, recording or any information storage and retrieval system, without permission in writing from the author.

Unless otherwise indicated, scripture quotations are taken from the Holy Bible, NEW INTERNATIONAL VERSION®, NIV® Copyright © 1973, 1978, 1984, 2011 by Biblica, Inc.® Used by permission. All rights reserved worldwide. Scripture quotations marked (AMP) are taken from the Amplified® Bible, Copyright © 1954, 1958, 1962, 1964, 1965, 1987 by The Lockman Foundation. Used by permission. Scripture quotations marked (ESV) are taken from The Holy Bible, English Standard Version® (ESV®), copyright © 2001 by Crossway, a publishing ministry of Good News Publishers. Used by permission. All rights reserved. Scripture quotations marked (NKJV) are taken from the New King James Version®. Copyright © 1982 by Thomas Nelson, Inc. Used by permission. All rights reserved. Scripture quotations marked (NLT) are taken from the Holy Bible, New Living Translation, copyright ©1996, 2004, 2007 by Tyndale House Foundation. Used by permission of Tyndale House Publishers, Inc., Carol Stream, Illinois 60188. All rights reserved. Scripture quotations marked (TPT) are taken from The Passion Translation®. Copyright © 2017, 2018 by Passion & Fire Ministries, Inc. Used by permission. All rights reserved. ThePassionTranslation.com. Scripture quotations marked (NASB) are taken from the New American Standard Bible®, Copyright © 1960, 1962, 1963, 1968, 1971, 1972, 1973, 1975, 1977, 1995 by The Lockman Foundation. Used by permission. Scripture quotations marked (TLB) are taken from The Living Bible copyright © 1971 by Tyndale House Foundation. Used by permission of Tyndale House Publishers Inc., Carol Stream, Illinois 60188. All rights reserved. The Living Bible, TLB, and the The Living Bible logo are registered trademarks of Tyndale House Publishers. Scripture quotations marked (VOICE) are taken from The Voice™. Copyright © 2008 by Ecclesia Bible Society. Used by permission. All rights reserved. Scripture quotations marked (CEV) are taken from the Contemporary English Version Copyright © 1991, 1992, 1995 by American Bible Society. Used by Permission. Scripture quotations marked MSG are taken from *THE MESSAGE*, copyright © 1993, 2002, 2018 by Eugene H. Peterson. Used by permission of NavPress. All rights reserved. Represented by Tyndale House Publishers, Inc. Scripture quotations marked (WEB) are taken from the World English Bible, which is in the public domain. Scripture quotations marked (NCV) are taken from the New Century Version®. Copyright © 2005 by Thomas Nelson. Used by permission. All rights reserved.

Print ISBN: 978-1-4866-2423-2
eBook ISBN: 978-1-4866-2424-9

Word Alive Press
119 De Baets Street, Winnipeg, MB R2J 3R9
www.wordalivepress.ca

Cataloguing in Publication may be obtained through Library and Archives Canada

Contents

	Getting Ready	xi
Day 1:	Transformed by the Power of Gentleness	1
Day 2:	A Gentle Whisper	3
Day 3:	His Greater Purposes	5
Day 4:	Stooping Down	7
Day 5:	Drop Those Stones	9
Day 6:	Sow for a Harvest	11
Day 7:	Out of the Cold	13
Day 8:	Finding Father	15
Day 9:	The Power of Words	17
Day 10:	Gentle Acceptance	19
Day 11:	The Real Deal	21
Day 12:	Under Wing	23
Day 13:	The Gentle Servant	25
Day 14:	The Melted Heart	27
Day 15:	A Culture of Gentleness	29
Day 16:	A Great Invitation	31
Day 17:	Stay Focused	33
Day 18:	"No matter what!"	35
Day 19:	Coffee Break	37
Day 20:	A Costly Fruit	39
Day 21:	Dangerous Driving	41
Day 22:	Guard Your Words	43
Day 23:	A Righteous Response	45
Day 24:	Working Together: Patience and Self-Control	47
Day 25:	Don't "Stuff" It	49
Day 26:	Ready, Set, Run!	51

Day 27:	Victory over Lies	53
Day 28:	No Revenge: Just Revival!	55
Day 29:	A Garden Wrestle	57
Day 30:	A Second Chance	59
	Small Group Helps	61
	Contributors' Biographies	71
	About the Author	77

These two aspects of love
—gentleness and self-control—
take strength, time, challenges, and patience to cultivate.
The evidence of the work of the Spirit has been before me daily
in the life of our daughter

Janelle May Wood

to whom I dedicate this book.
Whether entertaining the many neighbourhood kids wall-to-wall
in her home, serving on the school's parent council, teaching teenagers
to drive, or gently caring for her clients in the retirement home,
she sweetly, with God's help, models for all of us
gentleness and self-control.

Getting Ready

But the fruit produced by the Holy Spirit within you is divine love in all its varied expressions: joy that overflows, peace that subdues, patience that endures, kindness in action, a life full of virtue, faith that prevails, gentleness of heart, *and strength of spirit ...*
—Galatians 5:22–23, TPT (emphasis added)

But the fruit of the Spirit is love, joy, peace, longsuffering, kindness, goodness, faithfulness, gentleness, self-control. *Against such there is no law.*
—Galatians 5:22–23, NKJV (emphasis added)

Let's face it—engaging in a Christian walk characterized by gentleness and self-control can seem distasteful, weak, and certainly unappealing. Motivating talks more often highlight such vocabulary as armour, authority, power, and mountain-moving faith. But gentleness and self-control? Perhaps helpful when stroking a pet or saying "no" to sweets.

Gentleness, however, is a fruit of the Holy Spirit working in our lives and is not incompatible with justice, authority, faith, or righteous anger. Jesus invites us to partner with Him, "... *learn from me, for I am gentle and humble in heart ...*" (Matthew 11:29a). He isn't calling us to be feeble and powerless but submitted, teachable, and loving.

Biblically, we see gentleness related to courage, fortitude, and resolution. Paul was like a tender mother caring for and feeding her children (I Thessalonians 2:7). But when the Corinthians challenged his spiritual authority, he asked them: *"What do you prefer? Shall I come to you with a rod of discipline, or shall I come in love and with a gentle spirit?"* (1 Corinthians 4:21). He bore the fruit of the Spirit and knew both firmness and gentleness.

Consider the gentleness displayed by Jesus when He washed the disciples' feet, healed the sick, and prepared for the journey to the cross. Even while He hung on the cross, He spoke gentle words of forgiveness for those who had crucified Him.

When it comes to self-control or "strength of spirit," culture tells us, "Be yourself; tell them what you really think; learn to fight; if it feels right, it *IS* right." Self-control in scripture is strength within. It's the ability, with God's help, to govern our own behaviour. Paul uses "self-control" in 1 Corinthians 9:24–27 to describe an athlete who masters his emotions and his body in order to run a race. Self-control as the fruit of the Spirit is self-discipline.

Many scriptures point to self-control as bringing balance. All of our God-given powers, such as the capacity to reason, to feel, and to exercise our will, can be abused. That's why we need the Holy Spirit's help to cultivate self-control and bring balance in areas like control of the tongue (James 3:2), control of sexual desires (1 Corinthians 7), wise use of our time (Luke 12:35–48), and self-control in our thinking (Philippians 4:8).

Jesus was *"tempted in every way, just as we are—yet he did not sin"* (Hebrews 4:15b). This is self-control under the power of the Holy Spirit. A great picture of such self-control is found in Luke's account of the devil's temptation of Jesus (Luke 4:1–13).

Our Galatians 5 passage adds this:

> *Since this is the kind of life we have chosen, the life of the Spirit, let us make sure that we do not just hold it as an idea in our heads or a sentiment in our hearts, but work out its implications in every detail of our lives. (v. 25, MSG)*

I pray that these devotionals encourage you to continue to submit to the work of the Holy Spirit daily as you seek to cultivate gentleness and self-control.

Transformed by the Power of Gentleness

Day One

Remind your people . . . not to be rebellious. They must always be ready to do something helpful . . . They should be gentle and kind to everyone.

—Titus 3:1–2, CEV

In his book *Spirit Fruit*, John Drescher tells this story of the gentleness of the great evangelist D.L. Moody. Crowds would regularly line up to hear Moody everywhere he went. On one occasion, a young boy, dirty and ragged, came to the door of the church where he was to preach. The usher at the entrance took one look at him, refused him entry, and suggested he go home to bed. Devastated, the young boy went to the side wall of the church, sobbing. When Moody arrived in his carriage, he heard the boy's sobs and asked what was wrong. He explained that he wasn't allowed in to hear Moody preach. Moody smiled and said, "I know how you can get past that big fellow at the door. Are you willing?" The boy's response was a definite, "Yes, sir!"

Moody told him to hold on to his coattails and not let go until he said so. He walked into the church and up to the pulpit and put the boy in his chair, where he listened to Moody preach. The pastor who told this story explained, "The reason I know it is true is because it happened in my church, and I was that little boy." Moody's gentle handling of a crisis in this boy's life led him to become a full-time minister in that very church where the kindness was shown.[1]

This reminds me of another true story recorded in the New Testament in which a man was denied "attendance" and community because of his

---

1   John Drescher, *Spirit Fruit* (Scottdale, PA: Herald Press, 1974), 304.

physical condition (Matthew 8:1–4; Mark 1:40–45; Luke 5:12–16). Like the young boy, this man was very likely dirty and ragged but also covered with oozing sores. Leprosy was most dreaded because of its incurable and contagious character. In keeping with the law, leprosy was declared a judgement for sin, so lepers were unclean and unfit to participate in family, community, social, or religious activities.

Mark records the day when this leper, against both laws and protocol, having heard of Jesus' power to heal, approached Him and begged for His mercy, asking if He would be willing to make him clean. If the teachers of the law and the members of society had been a little more on guard with the surrounding activity, he would have been sent running. He certainly didn't fit the crowd that had come to see Jesus. But the leper approached Jesus:

> ... *imploring Him* ... *"If You are willing, You can make me clean." Moved with compassion, Jesus reached out with His hand and touched him, and said to him, "I am willing; be cleansed." And immediately the leprosy left him, and he was cleansed.*
>
> —Mark 1:40–42, NASB

What a beautiful, gentle touch and welcome that leper received. Jesus showed us who God is by loving one who had been judged and rejected. Jesus knew what touching a leprous man meant; nevertheless, He did it without hesitation. Clearly, love runs deeper than the law.

In both the young boy's and the leper's situations, we see how the power of a gentle, compassionate response transformed a life. Let's allow the fruit of gentleness in our lives to welcome those who need to reach Jesus. Our flesh may want to disqualify people for reasons that may seem reasonable or logical, but Jesus includes all—the ragged, the rich, the unclean, the unlearned, the oppressed, and the weary. Above all, He welcomes the hungry. Will we show who God is by loving in such a manner?

> *Jesus, I want to be ready to give a gentle welcome and an affirming touch to those whom you send my way. Help me to represent you well today and every day. In your name I pray. Amen.*

A Gentle Whisper

Day Two

Contributed by Sunita Ramadeen

Elijah was afraid and ran for his life . . . he went into a cave and spent the night. And the word of the Lord came to him: "What are you doing here, Elijah?" . . . the Lord is about to pass by." Then a great and powerful wind tore the mountains apart . . . but the Lord was not in the wind. After the wind there was an earthquake, but the Lord was not in the earthquake. After the earthquake came a fire, but the Lord was not in the fire. And after the fire came a gentle whisper . . . Then a voice said to him, "What are you doing here, Elijah?" . . . "Go back the way you came . . ."

—I Kings 19:3, 9, 11–13, 15

Guyana, Monday, September 19, 1983. My dad was enjoying an evening walk. By 9:00 p.m., he hadn't returned home. Then came the dreadful and devasting news. He had been struck by a car and succumbed to his injuries. He was thirty-six years old.

Sorrow, hopelessness, fear, and anxiety entered me for the first time. Our Hindu religion taught that this accident meant God was mad at us and didn't like us, so he killed my dad. That lie became truth to me. Already feeling unloved by God, custom dictated that we must cut family ties and become outcasts to my dad's relatives. While dealing with our grief, we had to find help from my mother's side in order to begin again. We relocated to the next village with my mom's elderly Muslim parents, entrenched in extreme poverty.

My broken heart longed for a God who would care and hear my prayers. I found myself searching for someone to ease the pain in my heart—looking everywhere, from the Muslim mosque to the Hindu temple. There was no answer and no help. He was not in the wind; He was not in the earthquake; He was not in the fire.

When I was invited to a Christian church, something was different. The presence I felt comforted my tattered heart. After the worship, the preacher spoke about Jesus' love. That evening, at home and alone in my room, I fell to my knees. I asked this Jesus to heal my heart and promised Him my loyalty for my lifetime. As He came into that room with me, He healed me with His love and freed me from the lies. His gentle whisper assured me that He'd never hated me.

I began sharing my experience boldly with my grandparents, Muslim relatives, and everyone I could. Many of my relatives got saved, which didn't go over well with my strong-headed and resistant Muslim grandparents and uncles.

I eventually migrated to Canada to live with my sister and her family. While praying one day, I heard that gentle voice asking me to go back to Guyana to visit. I didn't know why, but like Elijah, he was calling me to "go back the way I came." My devout Muslim grandfather became severely ill one week after I arrived. As I ministered to him, the presence of God filled the room. My grandfather rose up running, lifting his hands, and repeatedly shouting, "Thank you, Jesus!" He had a personal salvation encounter with Jesus that day and went home to meet Him two days later. Although my grandmother continued unwaveringly in her Muslim faith, the Lord allowed me later, during a second visit, to lead her to Jesus before she passed away.

He is so good. His gentle whisper can draw us close, heal us, and break the power of lies. That same whisper can also send us to those who still need to experience salvation and transformation, because each of us matters to Him.

Lord, I confess that sometimes all I hear is the noise, the confusion, and the lies. Help me to hear and obey your gentle whisper. In Jesus' name I pray. Amen.

His Greater Purposes

Day Three

Contributed by Mark Soppitt

"He will not crush the weakest reed or put out a flickering candle. He will bring justice to all who have been wronged."

—Isaiah 42:3, NLT

In 2005, I moved from the UK to Canada with a young family to pastor a church in Niagara Falls. Full of prophetic promises and direction, we were excited to start our adventure in a new country. However, we were soon overwhelmed with the demands of raising five young children in a very different culture. Furthermore, the church we moved to was more broken than we imagined, and those who'd remained after years of turmoil were exhausted. But with the energy of vision and faith, I began to pastor the church back into health and see it grow again.

New members were added for the first few years, and we saw God move in exciting ways. However, toward the end of 2008, I began to suffer from a deep and relentless depression. From exciting hope, I entered an inescapable, barren wilderness of hopelessness that would last for seven years. In 2009, I wrote in my journal, "How do I tell you that I want to die? ... I am afraid of the sentence of death that rings in my head, surrounded by loneliness and nothingness."

With the support of an amazing leadership team, I limped on as pastor. But my depression worsened, and in 2012, I attempted to take my own life. Through the next few years, I was hospitalized numerous times. My psychiatrist said I would never work again, and I believed him. But my wife, Janet, would not—she laboured hard, looking after our five traumatized children with little income and much pain.

In 2015, my health began to improve, and I found work in a factory. There God gently began to restore my soul. I began to worship, witness, and pray again. Having been terrified of people, I began to love and interact with others. I came to call this place my "Bethel," as it was the unexpected place where I repeatedly met powerfully with God.

We constantly saw God's provision coming through friends, family, church, counsellors, and unexpected sources. When we couldn't afford pizza for our daughter's birthday party, Janet found a $50 bill as she was walking and asking God to provide. When Janet learned that having a dog was good medicine for depression, God provided the perfect puppy, for free, the next day!

God has a sense of humour. During my illness, I miraculously became a fitness instructor at the YMCA! Even in my suffering, I look back and see Jesus taking me into our community, identifying and supporting many suffering people. Through my utter brokenness, I could see how much God loves to work His purposes as He restores the hurting simply through His love.

Isaiah's words above paint a beautiful picture of the heart of Jesus: He will not crush the weak reed but strengthen it to become a cedar in the courts of our God. He will not quench the flickering candle but will breathe upon it until it grows into a radiant flame. Jesus tenderly works beyond our flesh, taking His time because He is fashioning something beautiful and new. Then He teaches us how to express this powerful gift of gentleness to others.

God treats the one who is bruised and weakened with tenderness, inviting us to follow Him. His gentle work often requires our quiet trust as we walk through the challenges and mysteries of life. We clearly see Him protecting and rebuilding as we continue to seek God's complete restoration in our family. We trust Him and praise Him with every step.

Thank you, Lord, for breathing upon the flame of my heart when it's only a flicker. I see that in my weakness, you become my strength. Guard my heart as you so gently bring fresh life and restoration. In your name I ask. Amen.

Stooping Down
Day Four

You protect me with your saving shield. You support me with your right hand. You have stooped to make me great.

—Psalm 18:35, NCV

As adults, we seldom consider how our physical presence, structures, sounds, or authority figures impact those around us. Do you remember how big everything seemed when you were a child? Ferris wheels, trucks, trees, and certain adults. The adults whose presence was massive—the Queen, the pastor, the dentist, the police officers, the doctor!

Over time, we grow up and gain perspective. The Queen is special. The police officer is our protector, the pastor teaches us biblical truth, and the doctor reassures us when we're sick. They become approachable and appreciated. (Notice I have refrained from commenting on the dentist!)

I read recently of a young father who shared from his 6' 3" grown-up landscape:

> ... My wife reminds me that when I begin to lose my temper, I can be a bit scary for a child who's only a few feet tall. When I'm at my best as a parent, and one of my kids is beginning to struggle, the best thing I can do is kneel down on their level and speak to them in a soft, gentle voice. This is what God did when He sent Jesus to be among us."[2]

---

2 "Sermon Illustrations on Gentleness," The Pastor's Workshop, accessed May 8, 2023, https://thepastorsworkshop.com/sermon-illustrations-on-gentleness/.

Gentleness is an essential ingredient in good parenting. When we're gentle with our children, we help them to develop into well-rounded individuals who can navigate the challenges of life. By cultivating this fruit of the Spirit in our personal lives, we model God's character and give them the best possible foundation for a confident, happy, and successful future.

Even though we gain perspective about things that were out of reach and even somewhat intimidating for us as children, as adults we sometimes mistakenly think of God in a similar way. We may see Him as a massive, distant force angrily reminding us of how inadequate and defective we are. We find ourselves in chronic fear with a sense of failure. Those intimidating pictures from childhood linger, clouding the truth about the Father's approachability.

Psalm 18:35 says of our Heavenly Father: "... *You support me with your right hand. You have stooped to make me great* (NCV, emphasis added). David is saying that God reached down to help a modest, unpretentious shepherd boy become a king. In the same manner, in humility Jesus stooped down to become man to reconcile us to the Father. What a beautiful picture! *"Who is like the Lord our God, the One who sits enthroned on high, who stoops down to look on the heavens and the earth?"* (Psalm 113:5–6, emphasis added). We don't need to feel intimidated or overwhelmed. He is stooping to fulfil his plan and purpose for greatness in our lives.

Jesus, thank you for stooping down to bring me to the Father. Show me the truth of His gentleness and love for me today. Amen.

Drop Those Stones

Day Five

"Then neither do I condemn you," Jesus declared. "Go now and leave your life of sin."

—John 8:11

One of the greatest struggles in my Christian walk is second-hand offence. God has given me many practice runs to build my forgiveness muscle, and though very challenging and painful, I am grateful. I understand that when someone hurts me, forgiving is commanded. My ability to have a clear, unhindered connection to my Heavenly Father depends on it. I know it means choosing to walk in a higher realm, where someone else's attitudes, words, and actions don't dictate my attitudes, words, and actions. It isn't letting the other person off the hook or saying it was OK. It takes time, sometimes a long time, for the feelings to line up with the decision.

I recall my pastor telling someone that he was sure I would even forgive the devil. But do something nasty or speak something unkind to someone I love, and something wild and furious is unleashed in me. That's when every strategy to kill the flesh and walk in the Spirit is called into action. It's a time when I know my weakness and must depend on His strength.

In my closet chats with Jesus, I have visited His dealings with the woman recorded in John's Gospel, who was caught in adultery. I imagine her as a close friend. I wonder if she was even agreeable to the act. I feel my desire for revenge on the salivating crowd with their stones in hand. And I watch how Jesus responds.

Cultivating Gentleness and Self-Control

> ... *the Pharisees brought in a woman caught in adultery. They ... said to Jesus ... In the Law Moses commanded us to stone such women ... Jesus bent down and started to write on the ground with his finger. When they kept on questioning him, he ... said to them, "Let any one of you who is without sin be the first to throw a stone at her." Again he stooped down and wrote on the ground. At this, those who heard began to go away one at a time ... until only Jesus was left, with the woman ... Jesus ... asked her, "Woman, where are they? Has no one condemned you?" "No one, sir," she said. "Then neither do I condemn you," Jesus declared. "Go now and leave your life of sin."*
>
> —John 8:3–11

Jesus knew that she was guilty, but He saw beyond her reputation. He saw her need, and with gentleness, He restored her. He didn't give in to the Pharisee's attempt to trap Him. He was moved with compassion as He saw her humiliation and shame.

Gentleness works hand-in-hand with humility. Without that humility, we can become prideful and feel the need for revenge. To express the fruit of gentleness in our lives, we must not view ourselves as better than someone else. Rather than asserting self-righteousness, our desire must focus on bringing restoration without engaging in stone-throwing.

Jesus' response to the woman in this story reminds me that He's also gentle with us. He models a godly and loving response, showing us the strength of gentleness. Even in our sin, He continues to love us. He doesn't keep a record of our wrongs but offers forgiveness.

I'm learning to prayerfully ask God to help me with patience, self-control, and gentleness when tempted to hold on to second-hand offence. I've also asked Him to root out the self-righteousness and grow me in ways that best reflect His character. My pile of stones ready for those Pharisees must be left at the cross as I learn to walk the Jesus way.

> *Jesus, I am so thankful for the cross. In speaking freedom and forgiveness for this woman, you remind me of the gentle acceptance you offered to me so that I could be one of your family. With your help, I leave with you those stones I self-righteously hold. Amen.*

Sow for a Harvest

Day Six

So, as God's own chosen people ... put on a heart of compassion, kindness, humility, gentleness, and patience [which has the power to endure whatever ... unpleasantness comes, with good temper]

—Colossians 3:12, AMP

My mom was a 4' 11" giant of a woman who was, in many ways, ahead of her time. From the 1950s to the 1990s, she raised four challenging kids (and some additional stragglers), chaired women's church committees, kept detailed financial records for both the household and the church, served as self-appointed church historian, ran an alcohol rehab at her kitchen table, and mended and boxed up clothing every week for various mission agencies. While doing all of that, she managed to work outside the home with long-term employment in the local knitting mill, a toy factory, and a hotel, where she scrubbed floors (on her knees). She even advised the mayor on how to run the town at times, and since she'd been the one who had prompted his freedom from alcohol and led him to salvation, he occasionally listened. Love was the key to everything she undertook.

But slowly an illness began its deteriorative work. Her world became increasingly small. After the kids were married, well-settled in homes of our own, and bringing the tribe of grandkids to visit, her life became more of what she couldn't do and less of what she could do. She fought to convince us all that things were just fine for a long time, always with a gentle response and a sense of self-confidence. The long dried-out food supply in the fridge, the generous financial gifts to people we didn't know, and the many misplaced but "missing" items told us otherwise. While still the champion of laundry and meals for herself and our dad, she fought her loss of independence when we insisted on regular meal delivery. She considered offers to help somewhat insulting. However, her love for Jesus and people, her prayer times, and her well-worn Bible remained as constants. She was sowing for eternity.

After a move to a care home with good social interaction, much of her well-cultivated fruit of the Spirit began to bloom again. She endured most unpleasantness "with good temper," and joy was evident. She convinced the housekeeping staff that she should help change bedsheets "for the seniors," and they found she did superbly. Peace was evident; kindness was never lost. She had entrusted herself to the One she knew best, and her gentle, sweet smile told the story she could no longer speak.

Life wasn't as she planned, but she knew her Saviour would never leave her or forsake her. Throughout the transitions, we were able to walk with her, appreciating a mom who knew that she wasn't in charge of her destiny—a gentle woman who knew she didn't have to be in control, because God was. When others love us, it's easier for us to choose a path of humility, even in the most challenging circumstances. In an atmosphere of love, gentleness will thrive.

Paul wrote, *"Let your gentleness be known to all"* (Philippians 4:5a). It's hard to fathom at times, but this formerly violent and persecuting Saul of Tarsus had learned the gentleness of God. We sometimes doubt the power of gentleness, but history supports it in Matthew 11:28–29. Jesus says, *"Come to me... learn from me, for I am gentle and humble in heart, and you will find rest for your souls."* I wonder what our desperate world would look like if we entrusted ourselves to the One who knows us best, learned from Him, and cultivated the fruit of gentleness in our daily lives, anticipating a good harvest.

> *Heavenly Father, whatever unpleasantness comes, help me to meet it with good temper, kindness, and gentleness. Today I am entrusting myself to your grace, anticipating a good harvest. Amen.*

Out of the Cold

Day Seven

Contributed by David Pitcher

God's servant must . . . be . . . a gentle listener . . . who keeps cool, working firmly but patiently with those who refuse to obey. You never know how or when God might sober them up with a change of heart. . .enabling them to escape the Devil's trap, where they are caught and held captive, forced to run his errands.
—2 Timothy 2:24–26, MSG

The apostle Paul wrote these words when mentoring his young understudy, Timothy. A personal encounter made them a reality in my life.

It was the stormiest day of December in a small Ontario North community where my wife and I oversaw the Salvation Army Family Services. I had just left the Salvation Army building in the old van to pick up some donations for the Christmas hampers. The snow was deep, and very little traffic was moving.

Not far along on my errand, I noticed a hulk of a guy, obviously heavy-hearted, struggling to make his way up the street, a shopping bag under each arm. He seemed to be talking to the air, crying out for help. I stopped the van to see if I might be of help. Looking at me standing there in my uniform, he started walking toward me, and as he came closer, I heard him say, "You're just the one I need to see. Do you think you could say a prayer for me?" He had been crying out to God for someone, hopefully a pastor, to come along to pray for him. He felt hopeless and desperate.

Sensing his need, I invited him to sit in the van. It would be easier to talk and pray there. I climbed back behind the wheel and suggested we take time for some coffee and a donut. The church wasn't far, and he looked exhausted and maybe hungry. He asked, "Are you sure you're not too busy?"

I replied, "Nothing that can't wait. You'll feel a whole lot better."

Back at the church, the man, Don, was feeling a little better and had shared more about his situation, his inner pain, and his battle with depression. I prayed with him, trusting God to do much more than I could. I drove him to his home and invited him to worship with us on Sunday. He said he would, but I reflected on how many times I'd heard that promise. But God heard my prayer, and Don came to the church on Sunday.

As Don and I got to know each other during the Christmas celebrations, he started to put many things together in his mind. He had gone to Sunday school as a child back home in the prairies but had never really applied God's Word to his life. In time Don came to the Lord and experienced new life in Christ. A couple of verses were pivotal in his decision: "... *in all things God works for the good of those who love him*" (Romans 8:28b) and "*The Lord is my Shepherd, I lack nothing ...*" (Psalm 23:1).

Don's decision for Christ led to much new growth in his faith, and he became stronger daily. In his former life as a nightclub bouncer, he had to deal with problems of alcohol and many temptations of the flesh. Adjustments to the new lifestyle weren't easy, but he was learning that he needed God's love and the support of his new "family" in Christ. His appreciation for this new family was thrilling.

As he matured in Christ, Don said that the miracle of his conversion began that winter afternoon when he cried out to God, and I met him at that corner. God's love worked through gentleness, love, and acceptance that day, leading to a transformed life and a grateful heart.

Father, I'm excited as I invite you today to teach me how to be that gentle listener. May I experience the joy of helping others to escape the traps of the enemy and find freedom in you. In Jesus' name. Amen.

Finding Father

Day Eight

Contributed by Craig Forbes

Gently encourage the stragglers, and reach out for the exhausted, pulling them to their feet. Be patient with each person, attentive to individual needs.
—1 Thessalonians 5:15, MSG

For the majority of my life, I was fatherless. At nine, my sister and I came to Canada to reunite with my mother and soon met a stepfather who was distant and disinterested. Their marriage dissolved in my final year of high school, and my mother, sisters, and I were left homeless.

We located my grandparents on my father's side, and I was sent to live with them in New York City. I'd at last be meeting my birth father. I'd often dreamed about this day. I wondered what he would do when I saw him. While other family members received me with open arms, my expectation for that love and acceptance from my father was shattered. He greeted me coldly with, "I don't owe you anything." Over the next year, I came to know him as an alcoholic who was abusive to his parents, especially my grandmother, and I hated him for that. Feeling dejected, I returned to Canada to be with my mother and two sisters. We lived in government housing, where I was surrounded by pimps, prostitutes, drug dealers, and thieves.

Fast forward several years. I married a beautiful woman named Stacey, blended our families, and started doing life together in our own broken way. While Stacey was pregnant one year into our marriage, I surrendered my life to Jesus. For the first time in my life, I experienced the love of a father, and it radically changed my life. I had peace, acceptance, and a genuine love for others. But I was hardly prepared for a distressing phone call I will never forget.

My birth father, now in Florida, was dying of AIDS. My previous thinking would have been, *Good for him!* After all, the Bible says that a man who doesn't care for his family is worse than an infidel. (I Timothy 5:8). Instead, my heart melted with sadness and compassion for this "exhausted straggler," my father, and the deep anger was replaced with love. My father needed Jesus!

I travelled to the Miami hospice, where I saw a frail, withering man with a perplexed countenance. He didn't seem to know me, but I shared some family pictures, and we chatted. I asked him, "Dad, if you were to die today, where would you spend eternity?"

"Only God can know those things," he replied.

I shared the gospel and the assurance of eternal life in Jesus. When I asked him whether he was willing to surrender his life to Christ, his response was a clear, "Yes."

As a child, I yearned to be loved and held by my father. God now turned the tables, and I gently held my father in my arms the way I had always wanted to be held. We prayed the sinner's prayer together, and I knew the angels did a grand crescendo. With tears of repentance, he apologized for not being there for me, and I fully forgave him. I whispered, "Dad, we will have eternity together." Not long after, my father graduated to heaven.

How do I continue to live out I Thessalonians 5:15? Only in His strength. For the past five years, with His help, I've been building relationships with our migrant farm workers. I see the power of His gentleness and love crumble walls of fatherlessness, hurt, and mistrust. God has turned my mess into a message of hope: "*Consider the kind of extravagant love the Father has lavished on us—He calls us children of God!*" (I John 3:1a, VOICE). He is the perfect Father, and His love can re-order impossible situations.

Heavenly Father, you call me your child. I am accepted and loved by you. Give me a gentle heart of compassion as I share with others the good news of salvation. Amen.

The Power of Words

Day Nine

A gentle tongue is a tree of life . . .

—Proverbs 15:4, WEB

The words of the reckless pierce like swords, but the tongue of the wise brings healing.

—Proverbs 12:18

Words uttered with gentleness are expressed in soothing comfort over a child's scraped knee, a lullaby for a sick infant, or an "I'm so proud of you!" Soft, kind, gentle, and encouraging words from a believer can diffuse even the most hostile situation. These words convey the fruit of the Spirit—a sense of genuine care and concern, with His love at their source. These words are more likely to carve a pathway to productive conversation. Life-giving words pay dividends for Kingdom growth and purpose. They can lift a head that is bowed down with grief or discouragement, bringing hope and reconciliation. These are described in Proverbs 15:4.

Conversely, harsh and impulsive words often carry regret and can take a long time to heal. One careless statement can provoke disagreements in marriage, business, church, or casual relationships. We can feel attacked, and our natural response is to fight back. Angry words, sarcasm, accusations, and criticism raise our defences quickly and often escalate into crippling conflicts.

My Grandmother Dinnick never had to raise her voice to tell you how she felt. She never had to use derogatory words or criticism, even when correcting choices or behaviours. She demonstrated a quiet strength that flowed from a deep love for others and a hearty portion of patience, peace, and kindness. Her gentle words assured the heart that any mistake was out of character, and turning the ship with God's help would surely bring success.

During my early years in ministry, I had numerous opportunities for both lay and pastoral training from well-known pastors, teachers, and apostles from across the globe. I saw how gentle words can carry a powerful anointing to break the hardest of hearts. I'm so thankful for others—family, friends, and leaders—who demonstrated this fruit of the Spirit as they simply lived out life. They likely won't know how much it taught me about the power of gentleness. There was the pastor who spent many nighttime hours lifting up words of prayer as he gently stroked the head of a dying saint with no family to surround them, the uncle who, with words of encouragement, patiently tamed a rebellious teen, a friend who spoke nothing but gentleness to a physically challenged son who required constant care. Such modelling by other lovers of Jesus has helped me to sense the Father's heartbeat for His created ones in a more excellent way. I have invited the Holy Spirit to grow me in this area of gentleness in words, and He has afforded me many opportunities to share in His joy. Take time today to thank Him for those whose gentle words have made a difference in your life.

How are your words making a difference in the lives of others?

> I choose gentleness … Nothing is won by force. I choose to be gentle. If I raise my voice, may it be only in praise. If I clench my fist, may it be only in prayer. If I make a demand, may it be only of myself.[3]
>
> —Max Lucado

Jesus, I confess, it's hard to bridle my tongue, and sometimes things come out before I can measure their impact. Forgive me for the words I now regret, and fill me with your truth and love. I want to be known as one whose gentle tongue is a tree of life. In your name I ask. Amen.

---

[3] "Gentleness Quotes," Goodreads, accessed April 26, 2023, https://www.goodreads.com/quotes/tag/gentleness.

Gentle Acceptance

Day Ten

What do you prefer? Shall I come to you with a rod of discipline, or shall I come in love and with a gentle spirit?

—1 Corinthians 4:21

In Sunday school, we often sang about the "wee little man" who climbed into the tree. It was a great action song, sure to get restless kids up and moving. When I read Luke's account of Zacchaeus, I sometimes still like to picture him perched in his sycamore tree, waiting to see Jesus—hidden away in the knowledge of his failures. He had been made rich by his greed and knew he wasn't doing the right thing. He was an outcast from the temple and the synagogues, despised by his own people, a traitor and a thief. Zacchaeus's salary was an income supplemented by extortion. Because the Romans hired him, he was considered an enemy to the Jews. He also may have been mocked because he was short in stature. On all accounts, he didn't fit in.

When Jesus was passing through Jericho, Zacchaeus found a good spot with an unobstructed view. Jesus stopped when he saw him up in that tree. He could see something on the inside that others could not, and with kindness and compassion, He gently called him down. He announced to the crowd that He was going home with Zacchaeus. Upon the invitation of Jesus to come down, Zacchaeus made haste. The response to that invitation led to restoration and salvation for Zacchaeus (Luke 19:8–10).

In elementary school, Georgie was one of my favourite students. Through no choice of his own, he didn't fit in. His struggle with Tourette's syndrome allowed him to be integrated for one class per day, but the remainder of his day was spent with me in my "special education" class. Each year at the June graduation celebration, Georgie would graduate, once again, to "Teakle's class." There was never a "Mrs."—he always referred to me fondly by my last name.

Over time, with God's help, I learned what it took to help Georgie survive in the school community. He didn't receive a warm welcome, and some of his peers intentionally made the situation difficult. It required patience and perseverance, but Georgie had my heart.

The classroom bulletin board was the focal point in my room. I changed up the colours and regularly displayed updated student achievement. I did so knowing that the changes would not be hidden from Georgie's attentive gaze, and it would set him off. With two hands grasping the background of corrugated paper, Georgie would give a giant tug and clear the entire board. Eventually, he knew and I knew, that on those mornings, his job would be to re-pin the display and make a "happy picture" for Teakle. It didn't involve anything for Georgie other than an invitation—no reprimand, no judgement, just a confirmation of the plan. Georgie's display would be much less organized and aesthetically pleasing than mine, but that's the way it would stay. Georgie would point it out with pride to classroom visitors.

Georgie knew when he had messed up—he really wanted to please. His success with playground interactions was minimal, and he was anxious and unmanageable when any staff member would raise their voice. Georgie really helped me cultivate the fruit of gentleness and self-control. A gentle voice, for Georgie, brought reassurance and cooperation.

Perhaps there's someone in your sphere of influence who needs a gentle invitation to find comfort, restoration, reassurance, or salvation. The continued work of the Holy Spirit in our lives can strengthen us to do what we cannot do on our own. Commit today to grow in a love-filled acceptance and value for others that sees a greater goal.

Open my eyes, Lord, to see what you see in others. Help me to cultivate a gentleness of spirit that will bring restoration and peace. In Jesus' name. Amen.

The Real Deal

Day Eleven

Contributed by Davina Boerefyn

Abide in me, and I in you. As the branch cannot bear fruit by itself, unless it abides in the vine, neither can you, unless you abide in me.

—John 15:4, ESV

Don't insist on getting even; that's not for you to do. "I'll do the judging," says God. "I'll take care of it."

—Romans 12:19, MSG

John watched in shock as Jesus held the bloodied ear of Malchus. Peter stood beside him, brandishing the sword he'd used, ready to protect Jesus again. As the crowd glared menacingly, Jesus gently pulled Malchus closer to Him. With the finesse of the master creator, He held the severed ear by the side of Malchus's head. The crowd blinked in astonishment as Malchus stepped away, touching the ear that was now re-connected and complete. It was as if the few seconds when his ear had been severed had never happened (Luke 22:39–51)!

John's heart hammered in anger. How dare these scoundrels from the High Priest treat Jesus this way. The response of Jesus perplexed him even more. It would have served Malchus right had Jesus left him writhing in pain. But there was Malchus, smugly following the orders of Caiaphas, the High Priest. Soon John couldn't see the face of his beloved Rabbi as the crowd pressed in, seizing Jesus roughly.

Before I learned to walk in submission to the Holy Spirit, the thought of gentleness made me uncomfortable. Some situations just didn't seem to deserve it. After all, if I didn't assert my strength, who'd be my advocate? So there I was in tricky situations, asserting my strength left, right, and centre, like a bull in a china shop, and feeling miserable about it.

Then I learned the trick of fake gentleness, how I could "gently" manipulate the situation, getting my way. No one was the wiser for it—except the wisest being in the entire universe. And He started gently pricking my conscience!

As I realized how useless fake gentleness was, God started inviting me to a place of rest, a place of death to self! And that meant letting go of wanting things my way and instead abiding in Him! Slowly but surely, God peeled away layers of deception and misunderstanding on this particular fruit of the Spirit. The carnal concept of viewing gentleness as becoming a doormat. A deception of equating gentleness with timidity or, even worse, fear.

Though the journey is ongoing, what a marvellous revelation it is when God starts defining concepts as He renews our minds. As I look at the picture of Jesus that day, on the brink of His crucifixion, I see perfect power under perfect control.

As I learned to abide in God, I realized that I didn't have to struggle with my old tendencies of needing to assert control. When the urge came to "put someone in place," I could hear the call of the Holy Spirit to come to Him with it first. From this place of abiding, the response could be the real deal, the fruit of gentleness instead of strife. I am learning that abiding leads to surrender and a trust that develops from an experiential knowledge of the faithful character of God.

Gentleness takes great strength—it is not timidity. Neither is it a pretense of softness while the inside of the heart is hard. Gentleness places our strength under God's guidance, and it becomes a powerful tool for God's kingdom. Gentleness speaks the heart of Jesus to a hurting and out-of-control world.

Dear Lord, I want to move past trying to pretend with a fake gentleness. Teach me to abide in you and learn from you. I want to walk submitted to true Holy Spirit gentleness. Amen.

Under Wing
Day Twelve

Jerusalem, Jerusalem . . . how often I have longed to gather your children together, as a hen gathers her chicks under her wings, and you were not willing.
—Luke 13:34

It had been a long journey through Galilee, Samaria, and Judea—teaching, healing, controversy, and opposition. But Jerusalem was not far now. Some Pharisees interrupted Him with word of danger from Herod, alerting Jesus that He should leave the area quickly or risk death. But Jesus had work to do. His heart was filled with love, protection, and "spiritual hugs" that they would not receive. The people of Israel rejected the one man who could save them. In His heart is no contempt—just longing and sadness in the loss of what could have been.

This simile portrays the humble and gentle attitude of wanting to cover and protect others—the embrace of a hen for her chicks when she sees danger approaching. For each of us, being "under His feathers" is a safe place in the storm and a welcome in our journey.

As carriers of His presence, we're meant to display the fruit of gentleness and warmth to others. Gentleness is the opposite of harshness. People should feel "safe" in our presence.

Do you remember the Peanuts cartoon, where Lucy stands beside a tree, looking up and shouting to Linus? "What are you doing in that tree?"

Linus responds from the branches, "Looking for something." Then he adds, "Can you see Snoopy? We climbed up here together, but I don't see him now."

Lucy unsympathetically shouts up the tree, "Beagles can't climb trees."

The next frame shows Snoopy falling out of the tree on his head with a loud *klunk*. "You're right!" Snoopy concludes.

"You stupid beagle, what are you doing climbing around in a tree?" asks Lucy.

Snoopy's sore head is spinning. Linus interrupts from the tree, "Don't yell at him ... We're trying to find a strange creature in a nest."

Lucy walks off, saying, "You're both crazy! Go ahead and knock yourselves out! I couldn't care less!"

Snoopy, with his head still sore, says, "Rats, I was hoping for a hug!"[4]

You may remember a time when you felt that way—wounded and spinning out from a bad decision. At that moment, you really needed the warm, comforting, gentle feathers of the "hen" and not the "Lucy" lecture. You just needed to know that somebody still cared and that you mattered.[5]

Like Lucy, we're often quick to open our mouths with frustration and judgement. But God resists our prideful justifications for not being gentle to those we feel don't deserve it. In offering a hug, we're not offering approval for sin, and they may additionally need good counsel and wisdom. But we are offering safety and covering during their storm.

To be like Jesus, you must have an abundance of "gentle embraces" stored up and available. Sadly, like those in Jerusalem, not all will welcome your offer. But as you, with gentle compassion, lift their heads higher than their mistakes, they will see hope and better days ahead.

Jesus, I sense the longing of your heart to draw me close, and I say yes. I want to be ready to love like you, with compassion and encouragement, even when it may be rejected. Amen.

---

4 GoComics, accessed April 19, 2023, https://www.gocomics.com/peanuts/1972/07/20.
5 Adapted from David E. Leninger, "Hoping for a Hug," Sermons.com, accessed May 3, 2023, https://sermons.com/sermon/hoping-for-a-hug/1466956

The Gentle Servant

Day Thirteen

... Though He was in the form of God, He chose not to cling to equality with God; But He poured Himself out ...

—Philippians 2:6–7a, VOICE

It was before Passover, and Jesus knew that the time had come for him to leave this world and to return to the Father. He had always loved his followers in this world, and he loved them to the very end.

—John 13:1, CEV

Here He was with His twelve. Twelve men who weren't exactly paragons of virtue. They were a unique band who blundered their way through trying to follow Him. And after His significant investment, they would desert Him as He went to the cross. But Jesus had a choice, and He picked these ones. He was doing His Father's will and preparing twelve who would become world changers. And on the night before His crucifixion, the greatest teacher was still teaching.

John highlights that Jesus understood both who He was and His mission in this moment:

... during the meal Jesus got up, removed his outer garment, and wrapped a towel around his waist. He put some water into a large bowl. Then he began washing his disciples' feet and drying them with the towel he was wearing.

—John 13:4–5 CEV

Here the divine host became the slave. Humility was despised in the ancient world as a sign of weakness, but Jesus regarded humble service to others as an honourable act. After gently drying each foot, those same hands that nails would soon pierce replaced each sandal and tied the straps. Those eyes that would soon grow glassy from the pain gazed into the depth of each heart. This display of true humility captures a panorama of the fruit of the Spirit in the purest form. Out of His heart of love, we see patience, peace, kindness, goodness, and gentleness expressed.

One Saturday afternoon, ten of us met at Dorothy's for a prayer meeting. She was a humble pastor's wife who wanted to encourage us and have us pray for the church's needs. We sang along with a CD and each took a turn to pray. Dorothy slipped from the room as we neared the final prayers. She returned with a large basin of warm water and a velvety white towel. The atmosphere was curious, but there was a silent hush and a rich closeness of the Holy Spirit. Dorothy moved to Lena's side, asking if she might wash her feet. Lena was cautiously receptive but trusted Dorothy. She began to weep within seconds of that water being so gently and humbly scooped across her feet. Dorothy prayed a beautiful prayer of appreciation to God for Lena's life and asked God to hear her heart's cry for her family. She dried Lena's feet and then returned to her own chair. No one moved for minutes. Then one after another, various ladies carried out a similar washing for a friend in the group. It was an extraordinary spiritual experience that brought a renewed sense of vulnerability, biblical burden-bearing, and servanthood.

Gentleness with humility is an essential mark of all who are born of the Spirit. Though Jesus was gentle and humble, He wasn't indifferent about things that were wrong. God's anger is against sin and evil; it doesn't affect His love and compassion for us. This is divine gentleness. Jesus displayed it in the humble act of washing feet. May such an attitude identify each of us.

I'm reminded today, Lord Jesus, that the road to greatness in your Kingdom is a pathway of servanthood. Teach me to embrace with joy every opportunity to be a washer of dusty feet, a hugger of crying babies, and a cleaner of kitchens and closets. It's going to take some work to cultivate such gentleness and humility, but I'm willing, with your help. Amen.

The Melted Heart

Day Fourteen

Do you realize that . . . his extravagant kindness is meant to melt your heart and lead you into repentance?

—Romans 2:4b, TPT

Few cities had been as favoured as Capernaum, where some of Jesus' most extraordinary miracles were performed. There He also pronounced judgement on some arrogant and self-satisfied recipients of those miracles. It would seem natural that gratitude would lead to an embracing of the gospel message and true repentance, but many enjoyed their healing without choosing to follow Him. Their hearts were thankless and guarded.

Jesus gives a fresh invitation with a word of comfort and an offer of grace: "*Come to me,*" (Matthew 11:28). To come means to believe (Acts 16:31), to receive (John 1:12), and to open a door (Revelation 3:20). Jesus knew they were carrying heavy burdens, and with continuing grace, He called them to a change of mind and heart as well as a freedom that He alone can impart.

Pastor Scott Sauls tells a story about a church nursery worker (whom we shall call Gloria) who bumped into a first-time visitor named Janet, who had dropped her two boys off in the nursery one Sunday. After the service, while Janet was waiting to pick up her boys, Gloria privately and quietly let her know there had been some issues. Apparently, the boys had picked fights with other kids, and one had broken some of the nursery's toys. In front of a room filled with the remaining children and their parents, Janet gave her boys a good verbal spanking. Then, to the horror of all, she screamed in a frustrated voice, "S—T!" Red-faced and deeply ashamed, Janet grabbed her boys and promptly hit the parking lot. No one could really guess the root of her forceful response, but it seemed pretty likely that this visit would be their last.

He goes on to say, however, that Gloria called the church office that Monday and asked whether Janet had left her contact information. She had. "I gave (Gloria) Janet's address, and unbeknownst to me, she sent Janet a note. The note read something like this:

> Dear Janet, I'm so glad that you and your boys visited our church. Oh, and about that little exchange when you picked them up from the nursery? Let's just say that I found it so refreshing that you would feel freedom to speak with an honest vocabulary like that in church. I'm really drawn to honesty, and you are clearly an honest person. I hope we can become friends. Love, (Gloria).

Janet came back the following Sunday, and the next, and the next. A door that had seemed closed to her was opened by that simple note. It gave her courage to return, and Gloria and Janet soon became friends. Months later, Janet became the nursery director for the church!

When Janet shared her testimony, she included the underlying confession that at the time of that first connection with the church, she was a recovering heroin addict. Gloria's gentle handling of the situation set Janet on a pathway to hope, healing, and destiny.[6]

The extra effort to connect was expressed with gentleness and humility, and it melted Janet's heart. Who is waiting for your affirmation and invitation today?

> Heavenly Father, you see the heavy burdens we so often carry beneath the surface. Thank you for those who have opened a door for me to be real and to receive your forgiveness, acceptance, and hope. Help me to treat others with a gentle kindness that will melt their hearts. Amen.

---

6 Scott Sauls, *Befriend* (Carol Strea, IL: Tyndale House Publishers, 2016), 29–30.

A Culture of Gentleness

Day Fifteen

Contributed by Brittany Jeyaseelan

With tender humility and quiet patience, always demonstrate gentleness and generous love toward one another . . .

—Ephesians 4:2a, TPT

After a long thirteen-hour flight from Auckland to San Francisco, I stepped into the airport and thought, *It's so good to be back on American soil.* While I was so grateful for opportunities to travel around the world, there was nothing quite like being home in America.

Shortly after I returned from New Zealand, I was introduced to a man in Canada who was originally from India. Spoiler—he was the man I would later marry! Suddenly, my life expanded, and I was entertaining the many changes that may be ahead. I love to travel but never imagined setting down roots anywhere other than the land I loved, especially after working for over a decade in American politics. But God had an exciting and unexpected plan.

We were in our thirties, and we both had a determination to wait for God's choice for a partner. From the start, we were prayerfully considering whether we would spend the rest of our lives with each other. Not only were we asking the Lord for wisdom and discernment, but we were also asking each other lots of questions. From my perspective, the gentle, respectful, and intentional way he "checked me out" was confirmation that he was God-fearing and real. An answer to many prayers!

Memorably, during our second conversation, he asked if I'd be willing to move to a different state, a different country, or a different continent. Without hesitation, I replied, "Yes." While retelling the story, that may sound quite forward for a second date, but in the moment, it didn't feel that way at all. I had already had my own Genesis 24:58 moment. The Lord had encouraged me with the story of Isaac and Rebekah. With peace from the Lord, it was easy to say, "I will go." We both knew that there wasn't a reason to keep dating if we weren't open to whatever God had planned for our lives. For me, it would mean moving.

A culture of gentleness and care is the cornerstone of our relationship. We grew up on opposite ends of the earth, and we have a lot to learn from each other! As we blend cultures as a family, we need humility, gentleness, patience, and love. We recognize that one culture isn't superior to another. We can't have unity as a family if we each demand our own way.

We don't all experience the stark differences between Western and Eastern culture every day, but as we interact with people, sometimes of a different culture, we must draw on the fruit of the Spirit. Humbly honouring others is a way of expressing the love and nature of Christ.

As we value what each one brings to the table, we learn gratefulness and grace. It may be as simple as me making a downright delicious American full-deal breakfast for my life group, and my husband arriving home with some spicy, hot samosas! We make room for each other's uniqueness and sincerely appreciate them. It can begin at home.

I encourage you to evaluate how you're living out Ephesians 4:2. What is your approach at work? How do you interact with your neighbours? Your extended family? We all have the opportunity to walk in humility, gentleness, patience, and love every day. The Holy Spirit is our strength. We can't do this by simply willing it so. As we cultivate gentleness, we can bring the love of Jesus into the opportunities of each new day.

> *Jesus, you understand my awkwardness in how to interact. I want to appreciate and honour, in more tangible ways, others who are different from me. Teach me how, Lord, in the days ahead. Amen.*

A Great Invitation

Day Sixteen
Contributed by Allan Gallant

Come to me, all you who are weary and burdened, and I will give you rest. Take my yoke upon you and learn from me, for I am gentle and humble in heart, and you will find rest for your souls. For my yoke is easy and my burden is light.
—Matthew 11:28–30

My wife has a sarcastic nickname for me—she calls me "golden fingers." Not because what I touch turns to gold—that would be awesome. No, it's because anything I try to fix or make, I break or turn into something worse than it was. One of the reasons for this is that I tend not to be gentle. Actually, I should be called the Hulk, because I regularly smash and break things. Let's say I give fixing a decent effort, but if it doesn't fit, I make sure it does, no matter what the finished products look like.

Gentleness isn't my strongest characteristic when building or fixing things. It's something I struggle with, even with my grandchildren. When I play with them, my wife, their *gentle* Nannie, says to me under her breath, "Be gentle." I can be like the beast in *Beauty and the Beast*, when he tries to have Belle come down for dinner. He's about to yell at her, but Mrs. Potts encourages him to be gentle, so he tries to speak in gentleness. It doesn't turn out well.

Jesus is the epitome of gentleness. In these verses from Matthew 11, Jesus welcomes us. He is gentle and humble in heart and partners with us in our burden-bearing. We can struggle so much with the heaviness of the matters of life: sickness, grief, loss of employment, death, depression, anxiety, and so on. These matters cause a lot of turmoil and hardship. I knew that struggle after a stroke and a diagnosis of clinical mental illness, I wanted to take my own life. I felt so broken and dead on the inside. In those moments, life can feel burdensome and laborious.

Many know this too well. The load you carry is just too oppressive, and at times you feel crushed under the weight of it. You feel broken, and the more you try to fix it, it only gets worse. It seems like you're being tossed on the roughest seas, and you long for a peaceful, safe place to land. There is the distant dream of a gentle cushion where you can find rest and healing.

There is good news. We have this *great invitation* to rest in the gentle yoke of Jesus, where we can heal and find peace. A place where we're carried and the heaviness of life is shouldered by Him. Why trust myself, trying to find comfort on my own or fix my mess, when Jesus stands ready to help? He won't just jam the pieces of my life back together—He will actually restore me! He will receive me and shoulder my cares through His gentle words and presence.

"Come to me" is a great call to your soul, to your inner world. A call to healing and rest. It's okay to put away the Hulk and the Beast and allow Jesus to care for you gently. Enter into His invitation. Release your grip on that which keeps you burdened and, like me, let His yoke of gentleness become that cushion to rest upon you while you heal and are restored.

Jesus, there are days when I think I'm the ultimate fixer, and I try to do things on my own. Thank you for the reminder that you are there to ease my burden and help me carry the load. Teach me how to release my grip and enter into your rest. Amen.

Stay Focused

Day Seventeen
Contributed by Kathy Mullen

Turn me away from wanting any other plan than yours. Revive my heart toward you.

—Psalm 119:37, TLB

Have you ever been working in the garden, concentrating on getting those weeds out or the flowers planted, and a pesky fly keeps buzzing around your head? It lands on your cheek, then whizzes past your ear, then your forehead, and on it goes. If this were a Saturday morning cartoon, the progression of scenes would be something like this:

Fly buzzes past gardener's face.

Gardener waves his hands around. Happens again.

Gardener gets up and waves his arms around—it's futile.

Close-up view of fly with dastardly intent in its eyes as it aims for gardener's nose.

Gardener swats his face, which makes him angry because that *hurt!*

Gardener gets up and chases the fly, again to no avail.

Next, Gardener grabs his shotgun and starts firing everywhere he spots the fly, tearing up the garden where he was working, breaking the windows in the house, dinging the car, putting holes in the neighbour's roof, and so on—you get the picture.

That picture depicts how a minor irritant can blow up into a major incident. When I overreact, small things can get under my skin to the point where I can lose self-control and "blow up the peaceful garden." Can you relate?

It can be particularly frustrating when we're working toward a goal and we get distracted by others, either intentionally or unintentionally. When the kids were small, it felt like they waited specifically for the moment I sat down to call someone or read something before they decided to test the rules, thwarting my best-laid plans. It was hard not to blow up at them, and I'm not sure my success rate was high. Fatigue and self-control will often oppose each other.

In Nehemiah 4, Nehemiah had a task to do—rebuilding the walls of Jerusalem that had been rubble for over one hundred years. The Lord commissioned him to build these walls, even giving him the king's backing to accomplish the work in a timely matter. However, some neighbours weren't on board but were opposed to the walls being rebuilt. The walls threatened their authority. They had laid claim to this territory, so they set out to stop Nehemiah. They tried to "negotiate" with him, and when the trickery failed, they decided it was time to attack.

Nehemiah heard of their plans and armed the workers on the wall. He knew that if he stopped to fight, the workers would be distracted from their goal, and the momentum would be lost. He set a plan in place for defence and then proceeded with his mandate. Nehemiah demonstrated what self-control looks like when there's a direct attempt to dissuade, distract, and deride you. He submitted to a higher call, which required his loyalty.

We may experience occasions when we could take the bait and get involved in discussions, gossip, or other distractions that divert us from the path we're intended to be on. As we cultivate the fruit of self-control in our lives, the Holy Spirit teaches us to remain focused. In that way, we don't lose sight of what we're called to do or who we're called to be. When we spend less time swatting flies and listening to the voices of distraction, we can be focused on our part in building the Kingdom of God. Self-control means finding the higher perspective, aligning with God's plan, and knowing the ground-level attack won't succeed in taking us off course.

Jesus, I'm reminded of the many times I have taken the bait. Help me to cultivate this fruit of self-control so that I don't lose sight of your purposes. I want to remain focused on what you have called me to do. Amen.

"No matter what!"

Day Eighteen
Contributed by Nicole Warden

Beloved friends ... surrender yourselves to God to be his sacred, living sacrifices ... For this becomes your genuine expression of worship ... be inwardly transformed by the Holy Spirit through a total reformation of how you think. This will empower you to discern God's will as you live a beautiful life ...
—Romans 12:1–2, TPT

The voice on the other end of the phone left me startled! "The X-ray shows a 4.5 x 9 cm. spot on Bob's lungs. You need to go to the hospital and ask that they do a CAT scan. I'll send the information ahead of you."

We alerted our pastors, friends, and family for prayer, then headed to the hospital. By the end of the day, the scan of Bob's lungs had come back clear—no cancer, no shadows, nothing but what we were previously aware of. How grateful we were for that news! The internist, though, had found the oxygen level in Bob's blood was tremendously low, and he needed to be admitted right away to receive oxygen and further tests. After nine days in hospital, Bob returned home accompanied by the invasive, constant cacophony of an oxygen concentrator. Bob was attached by hose to this machine 24/7. Oxygen canisters were made available for appointments.

Bob and I had been married for forty-six years. We did everything together—yard work, housecleaning, dishes, dog walking, grocery shopping. Yes, together. Now everything was left to me, with the additional task of caring for Bob. I could do so with love, but the emotions of this sudden change and the accompanying losses were overwhelming.

Not only was there the impact of the change in Bob's health and ability, but the reality of the situation brought deep dives that would catch me off-guard. My thoughts would spiral out of control. The thought of losing Bob, the paralyzing demands of life, the many nights of little sleep as I checked constantly to make sure he was still breathing—I was exhausted! I was losing my grip, often hiding to release the emotions, not wanting Bob to feel badly.

Amidst it all was an awareness of my need to lean into God. Having been through depression in the past, I was aware that in the turmoil, I needed to take every thought captive and remain constantly dependent on Him. I needed the fruit of the Spirit in self-control, but I was weak and in a fight to maintain some sense of normalcy. Like the psalmist, I cried, *"Lord, my heart is overwhelmed, lead me to the rock that is higher than I"* (Psalm 61:2, paraphrased).

One morning as I was pouring my heart out to God, I heard Him say: "Nicole, *no matter what*, you'll be okay." Those words settled me to the core of my being. I knew that I knew I would be okay. Whether Bob was with me or not, God would always be with me. This sunk deep into my heart. His response gave me the strength I needed to be fully surrendered, and my surrender at that moment became my act of worship.

What has changed? Very little on the exterior. Bob remains on oxygen except when sitting quietly. We've begun to do things together as his strength allows. But my thoughts no longer dwell on the situation, and I'm surrendering every question to Him moment by moment. That's the real key to self-control—giving Him control! That's when we're no longer tossed about by changes, circumstances, or negative reports, and we find peace in His presence.

I remain anchored by renewing my mind in His Word. I'm allowing the Holy Spirit to grow me in every fruit of the Spirit, including peace, patience, gentleness, and self-control. My heart remains established. I am confident that whatever is before us, we (like the three Hebrew boys) will be okay "no matter what!"

Father, you are reassuring my heart today that there is a peace in surrender. I'm inviting you to lead. Accept my surrender as my sincere act of worship today. Amen.

Coffee Break

Day Nineteen

Like a city that is broken down and without walls is a man whose spirit is without restraint.

—Proverbs 25:28, WEB

The rain early in the day had flooded the back yard, making outdoor play impossible. My husband, Carl, had left for work at 8:00 a.m. By 11:00 a.m., I was done! The Lego box had been emptied randomly across the dining room floor. Clean clothes from the rec room had made their way back to the wet laundry tub. Two remaining sippy cups from breakfast had become a meandering stream in the hallway.

Placing Cheerios, crackers, and grapes in my carry bag, I called "the tribe" and loaded all seven of them into the family station wagon. Station wagons held an unlimited number of kids, and seatbelts weren't a thing back then. McDonalds would be my saving grace to regain sanity.

Two were there because I had valiantly birthed them, and the other five were foster placements. What an international photo shoot—my two wispy white blondes, a red-haired three-year-old, a four-year-old with a silky, caramel-coloured mane, and the three African-American brothers with tight black curls. Seven little bumpkins, all six and under! I was able to utilize their supply of highchairs and boosters to seat everyone together. I put my six-year-old on guard and purchased my much-needed cup of coffee and some extra treats from the counter. I returned to the table, relieved.

Things were relaxed; the kids were behaving. Two gray-haired ladies nearby were engaged in a somewhat loud conversation due to apparent hearing deficits. With utter shock, I overheard one of the ladies say, "She's really been around." Her friend responded, "I don't know why they don't do something about people like that who run the streets." A hurricane of insult immediately churned within. They were talking about me; after all, many fathers were represented amongst my tribe. This was the last straw. How dare they! Under my breath, I rehearsed the choice words I had for them, along with my plan of action, and I stood up, ready for battle.

I'd like to tell you that at that moment, the Holy Spirit reminded me to turn the other cheek, buy them muffins, and send them home with a blessing, but what I remember was my need for revenge. I can't identify what prompted me to sit back down in my chair and stay silent, but I know it was something beyond my willpower. I could have made an excuse for my actions and the words I was about to say. The world lends validity to excuses. But how can our Sunday morning worship suddenly change to plans for payback when something strikes us the wrong way? I was ready with hurtful words—not to mention the cup of coffee I planned to "accidentally" spill over them. It shouldn't be that easy for us to switch gears.

Looking back, I realize it wasn't just what happened at that moment but what had been happening daily as I grew in the fruit of the Spirit. Little by little, God was giving me strength in places that were simply too difficult for just willpower. Self-control was the guard rail protecting me from a dangerous reaction I'd regret later. It was keeping me from straying into an area that was off-limits for the Spirit-controlled Christian.

We are partakers of the divine nature, and because of that, there's always a way out. Self-control isn't about self-mastery but Spirit sovereignty. The fruit of the Holy Spirit is being cultivated in us as we learn submission. We're meant to display the character of Christ, especially in the challenges. Then our lives can remain fresh and appealing to both God and man.

> *Jesus, I don't want to be a person without restraint when the challenges come and the flesh wants to fight. Thank you for the guard rail that keeps me from going off-limits into places of regret. Purify my heart and teach me how to submit to your sovereign ways in my life. Amen.*

A Costly Fruit

Day Twenty

Contributed by Misty Duggan

> God's Spirit doesn't make cowards out of us. The Spirit gives us power, love, and self-control.
>
> —2 Timothy 1:7, CEV

Life's landscape for me has been an abstract painting of darks and lights, highs and lows, and some steep learning curves. Some of the most pivotal situations in my life have been when I have exercised the fruit of self-control. As a people-pleaser and introvert who doesn't like conflict, it's hard for me to stand up for what's right—I don't like it at all. My heart races, and my throat closes up, but God's strength kicks in and helps me to choose what's right. Mentors have called it a "pure heart." I've always believed that God found me at a very young age and set me apart for Him. While I've always loved Him and tried to serve Him well, it's not been an easy journey.

I hate injustice, and when others have been unjustly treated, the strength to stand up for them overrides my fear of conflict, and the hidden lion in me finds its voice. When it's for myself, it's more challenging. My go-to in a situation when I need to stand my ground is to go into fight-or-flight, with an emphasis on flight to avoid making someone unhappy or angry. Following my convictions at the cost of not going along with the crowd, friends, and co-workers isn't easy. I've often been labelled as goodie-two-shoes, higher-than-thou, prude, innocent, and naive. Sometimes it's a very lonely spot.

To be clear, self-control, like any other fruit of the Spirit, comes at a cost. Love costs, peace costs, kindness costs—you get it. I know because I've had to count the cost personally. Saying no to someone and not going along with an ungodly decision cost me my career, dreams, and passion. It was a hard choice, a line in the sand, and when the other person remained relentless in moving forward and I didn't, there was no going back. Not everyone practises self-control at the same level. The lines can get blurry and cause interpersonal challenges for a Christian. Not everyone has the same convictions. Cheating the boss, over-spending, walking in biases, and opting out of personal integrity are often acceptable, since we have the "grace" card. Christians can even *plan to* disobey biblical standards by saying God will forgive. But God's Word is clear—forgiveness is not permission to sin.

I'm grateful that the fruit of self-control has protected me from making some of the biggest mistakes in my life. Jesus was beaten, spit upon, and betrayed by those closest to Him, so He set the bar high! Even considering the cost, He has been more than faithful to me.

If you feel the pressure to make choices you know aren't pleasing to God, even if you seem to be the only one choosing the right path, He will always be there for you, ready with the comfort and reassurance of His presence. He will be the warmth and acceptance you feel when you cry out to Him. He will be the unexpected peace in the deepest valleys. When you feel like you're drowning, His strong hand will pull you up out of the water and hold you close. Through the power of the Holy Spirit, you will move beyond your fear to trust His power and love.

My journey continues as I press toward the plans and purposes He has for me. With every victory, the glory is His. Daily I see how His goodness has been chasing me down. In God's economy, nothing is wasted. Today He reminds you, as He reminds me, *"God's Spirit doesn't make cowards out of us. The Spirit gives us power, love, and self-control"* (2 Timothy 1:7, CEV).

Holy Spirit, Show me any places in my life where the lines have blurred. I choose to move beyond fear and intimidation, selfishness, and sin to trust your power and love. In Jesus' name. Amen.

Dangerous Driving

Day Twenty-One

I do not understand what I do. For what I want to do I do not do, but what I hate I do.

—Romans 7:15

It's not easy to turn from temptation. When that cheesecake in the refrigerator is calling your name, when pornographic websites are just a click away, when that co-worker is pushing your buttons and you want to let them have a piece of your mind, it's not so easy to function with the fruit of self-control. Self-control, according to scripture, is a strength within—a work of the Spirit in our lives rather than rules and reminders from some outside source.

I heard recently of a young driver addicted to video games. He was caught on dash cam driving his Tesla on a busy highway while playing a game on the dash. Tesla officials say the feature was added to help drivers pass the time while their cars are docked in charging stations. But this driver was playing the game from behind the steering wheel while en route, endangering every traveller on that highway. Although a warning comes on the screen that it shouldn't be used while driving, the driver had chosen the "I am a passenger" setting. (Side note: Complaints prompted Tesla, in 2021, to add a locking setting while the car is in motion.)

Self-control is always for a greater purpose. A good father governs his tongue so that his children are raised in an atmosphere of safety, feeling valued and secure. An athlete masters their body and mind in order to win the race. A single person restrains their sexual desires so that they may fully enjoy sexuality in marriage. To allow people to travel safely to their destination and enjoy life, a person doesn't give in to the selfish desire to feed an addiction while driving. Sadly, without wisdom and restraint, we are all reckless drivers on the road of life.

Self-control directs us to the right choices. We know the dangers of choices such as overspending, overeating, losing our temper, committing adultery (even in our imaginations), and choosing screen time over Word time. We promise ourselves we're not going to do those things again. But sometimes, the pain or temptation is too great, and we give in.

Paul struggled with self-control as recorded in Romans 7:15–18:

> *I do not understand what I do. For what I want to do I do not do, but what I hate I do ... it is sin living in me ... For I have the desire to do what is good, but I cannot carry it out.*

Paul puts his finger on the real culprit—indwelling sin. When sin becomes a stronghold, no matter how much we want to do the right thing, we're checkmated. We can't follow through. Trying to wrestle that sinful nature to the ground by gritting our teeth and trying harder is a losing battle.

Winning in this battle means yielding to those greater purposes of God in our lives, and it takes surrender to the Spirit. A good starting point is in our minds: "... *believers, whatever is true, whatever is honorable and worthy of respect, whatever is right and confirmed by God's word, whatever is pure and wholesome, whatever is lovely ... think continually on these things ...*" (Philippians 4:8, AMP). A renewed mind will alert us quickly to the enemy's lies and guide us toward truth. Our will and emotions can then, with God's help, respond to that truth, and the fruit of self-control becomes the champion. As you drive through life surrendered and obedient, you can do so wisely and safely.

Where is there a battle for control in your personal struggles with sin? Begin the journey to freedom with a fresh surrender today.

> *Holy Spirit, it's true. Just trying harder doesn't work. The struggle is real. I want to travel this road of life with focus, obedience, and wisdom. I choose surrender and begin again in Jesus' name. Amen.*

Guard Your Words

Day Twenty-Two
Contributed by Caleb Courtney

Let everything you say be good and helpful, so that your words will be an encouragement to those who hear them.

—Ephesians 4:29b, NLT

Her tears took me by surprise. I couldn't remember making my mother cry before. In fact, I couldn't even remember the exact words I'd just said, though I knew they were incisive and cutting. I had thought we were simply matching wits, her clever wit against mine. I was about twelve years old. "Do you know that your mother is affected by the words that you say?" she asked through her tears. I shook my head. It sounds foolish now, but I didn't think my words had that much power. Mom always seemed so confident. Besides, we had such a loving family. How could she possibly believe a few mean words said with sarcasm?

I blushed. "I'm sorry, Mom. I didn't mean to hurt your feelings." We made things right, and in the end, I learned an important lesson: the words we say can profoundly affect others.

A decade later, I was in the middle of a crowd at a young adults' gathering in a church lobby. These were friendly people, and we all enjoyed being together. We got laughing, and I was making a few jokes. One of the guys said something funny, and I couldn't resist turning the joke back on him. My one-upmanship resulted in borderline hysteria. I enjoyed the attention. As I looked around the group, I noticed that absolutely everyone was laughing—everyone, that is, except the guy I had insulted in jest. He had a smile on his face, but his eyes told a different story. I could tell that my words had stung him. At home that night, I resolved to learn from this situation. "Lord," I prayed, "help me to use my words only to encourage and build up others."

The change didn't happen for me all at once. Once again, an opportunity arose in the middle of the good-natured young adults' group the following week. Someone made a seemingly innocuous comment about themselves. The words immediately popped into my head. It was a perfect sarcastic joke—biting, funny, and with just enough truth that everyone would see my observation's irony and hilarity. I imagined the fun of seeing everyone burst into laughter at my quick-witted comment. Then I remembered my resolution and prayer from the week before. I had already been trying to speak only edifying words to others at work, school, and home. I had come to realize that the same small nugget of truth that would make a sarcastic joke so funny was often the same thing that could genuinely uplift a person. In this moment, it came to me, and instead of using sarcasm, I affirmed the person.

There was no boisterous laughter. A few in the group had come to expect some quick wit from me and looked surprised but began to nod their heads. "You are good at that," one of the others commented to the person. "Yes, that's true," affirmed another. The attention wasn't on me. I looked around the crowd for smiles. Yes, some people were smiling. The biggest smile, though, was on the face of the person we had just affirmed; their eyes sparkled with life. What a contrast from the week before. Every person left that night feeling better than when they came.

Our words matter—they can tear people down or build them up. They can discourage or encourage. With God's help, I want to be an encourager. It's a lesson I'm still learning, and I'm inviting the Holy Spirit to help me cultivate this fruit of self-control in my words.

> *Heavenly Father, help me to guard my speech so that I speak words that line up with your Word. I believe that my words are meant to carry your truth and bring life to the hearers. Make me more mindful of each word I speak. Help me to eliminate idle and hurtful words so that I can be a blessing to others. Amen.*

A Righteous Response

Day Twenty-Three

Abram said to Lot, "Let's not have fighting between us... After all, we're family."
—Genesis 3:8, MSG

Abraham and Lot, who have travelled together since Ur, find themselves in Canaan in a tense and problematic situation in which some choices must be made. The scene is set in Genesis 13. A conflict arose between Abraham and Lot. They both had been blessed with more than they needed. Each of them possessed many flocks, herds, and tents. Their abundance of animals had strained the land and caused strife between the two groups of herdsmen. In fact, it had caused such a problem that they realized they would need to divide camp. This would solve the grazing area shortage for the many animals and prevent a confrontation among the herdsmen. But all of the lands had been promised to Abraham.

Abraham knew that he'd be better not being *with* Lot than being at odds with him. He wanted to keep peace in the family while ensuring that Lot had sufficient vegetation to feed his animals. He wasn't going to send his nephew back to Haran. Led by his generous and conciliatory heart and trust in God, Abraham subdued the flesh, though the lands were rightfully his, and gave Lot any piece of land he selected. He didn't want to make this a battle. He chose not to respond impulsively or in anger, with his pride or entitlement taking a front seat. Abraham chose to direct his attention to a solution to resolve the conflict. Solomon's wisdom instructs us, *"A hot-tempered person stirs up strife, but the slow to anger calms a dispute"* (Proverbs 15:18, NASB).

Cultivating Gentleness and Self-Control

We live in a day when self-control is a commodity in deficit. We need an abundance of God's help to learn how to be slow to anger, make wise choices, and act with a deep love for humanity. People are angry. Anger over police violence and racism is running high. Anger is provoked by the responses of politicians to debt, health care, and economic instability. People are ready to attack public officials for everything from food prices to speed cameras. Cancel culture is rampant for anyone who doesn't see things the "right" way. It's rare but beautiful to encounter a peacemaker who focuses on a solution.

While we're not meant to be silent in situations of injustice (Micah 6:8; Isaiah 1:17), we don't always have to get our own way to solve a conflict. We can learn a lot from men and women in the Bible by watching their choices and the consequences that result. In fact, the quicker we submit to the work of the Holy Spirit in releasing the fruit of self-control, the faster many situations can be resolved.

Abraham kept his emotions and desires under control in what could have become a nasty situation with Lot. Abraham trusted that God would make good on His promises, and he didn't need to fight with Lot for what he preferred. What a great picture of contentment and trust! Abraham refused to allow anything self-serving to become a priority over his love for a person.

The battle between obeying God or indulging our flesh is a high-stakes struggle with only one winner. But with the Holy Spirit on our side, we're equipped with self-control. Our self-effort will always fall short. Victory will come by getting to know the will of God, the voice of God, and the ways of God. In that place, we can function with our thoughts, words, and actions aligned with His.

Father God, your Word says that a fool will jump at the opportunity to quarrel. I ask you to give me wisdom to refuse to function in ways that are self-serving. I choose right relationship over my need to be right in a dispute. I choose to be a peacemaker and a friend with your help. Amen.

Working Together: Patience and Self-Control

Day Twenty-Four

Better a patient person than a warrior, one with self-control than one who takes a city.

—Proverbs 16:32

The art of self-control has much to do with not being impulsive or acting hastily. This is where patience comes in. Being patient and self-controlled helps us to weigh our actions and consider the possible outcomes. Sometimes we grow in these areas by observing the wise choices of others, and at other times, we learn well by observing where it is lacking. These situations teach us how not to do it!

Growing up, my three risk-taking, mischievous brothers helped me understand the consequences of having no patience and little self-control. When they had an impulse to do something, there was no consideration for consequences and no waiting. Whether it was brush painting Dad's Volkswagen fire-engine red while he was at work, reconfiguring the black, oily parts of a car engine on the kitchen table, or impatiently leaving Sunday service during the altar call to do power turns (donuts) in the gravel parking lot, they were up for it! (Waiting until they were licensed to drive would have been an aggravation.)

One of the more inventive games was stealing packets of vegetable seeds from the local grocer and selling them to families in the neighbourhood. The "large" income they received would have been good enough for anyone else, but not for them. They waited until the vegetables were in full bloom and then snatched them after dark from the well-nurtured gardens nearby and sold them door-to-door, sometimes to the same people from whom they'd stolen them. (Yes, they have since repented, but they did spend the money.) It was simply a way to supplement their small allowance, for which they would have to wait until the month-end. They wanted money *now!*

I've sometimes imagined what might have happened had any one of them been served up the expectation demanded of Jacob in Bible times. In the pursuit of a wife, Jacob's ability for self-control and patience was exemplary. His father, Isaac, had blessed him and sent him off to Haran to find the right woman. He was captivated by a young woman he met at a well, Rachel, the daughter of his Uncle Laban—it was love at first sight. Within a month, Jacob knew he must ask her father's permission to take her as his wife. Rachel had won his heart. Jacob and Laban agreed that Jacob would serve for seven years to gain this beautiful bride. Seven years! For most searching young men, that would be more than they could bear, but love partnered with patience, and those seven years seemed to Jacob like only a few days. Incredible!

When the seven years had passed, the conniving Laban provided a great wedding feast. Awakening the morning after the wedding, Jacob realized that he was the victim of Laban's deceit. He had spent his wedding night with Rachel's sister, Leah, and his heart was broken. Devastated, he confronted Laban. Laban insisted that he stay with Leah for the full week of her marital festivities, according to the custom of the days, and then he could have Rachel, but at a new price. Another seven years! That wouldn't stop Jacob. Patience and self-control would work within this man of principle and character, and the prize would be his treasured bride.

Delaying gratification in any area of our lives is no easy task. When we turn to Christ in faith, He places His Spirit within us to lead and empower us. Even though we are His, chances are there are still habits, desires, and impulses within us that fight for control. But with a moment-by-moment surrender to the Spirit and obedience to His Word, God promises victory.

Holy Spirit, I'm so glad that you wait patiently for us as we learn to walk with you. I invite you to lead me. I need your fruit of self-control, and I need renewed patience for today's journey. In Jesus' name. Amen.

Don't "Stuff" It

Day Twenty-Five

So prepare your minds for action and exercise self-control . . . Don't slip back into your old ways of living to satisfy your own desires. You didn't know any better then. But now you must be holy in everything you do, just as God who chose you is holy.

—1 Peter 1:13–15, NLT

Peter knew how easily we can be distracted, wasting time and energy in pursuit of the wrong goals. Even though we're walking with Christ, without self-control, we can slip back into bad habits and old ways. The struggle for self-control goes on inside an individual, but the results of self-control, or lack thereof, show up on the outside.

Over the years, I've enjoyed teaching many participants in my "Clutter Free" group sessions. Many Christians struggle with the over-acquisition of "stuff." The evidence can be found in garages, bedroom closets, corners of home offices, living rooms, and basements. Children's toys and objects spill from their shelves into living areas, kitchens, and bathrooms. Valued spaces are out of control—chaotic and overcrowded. Desires have gone well beyond need, and spending appetites have put many in debt.

Many people express frustration over wasted time searching for their keys, shoes, wallets, and other household items. They are often the same people who don't believe they have time to organize or set up systems in their homes that would bring peace and better stewardship of time and space. The irony is that more organized people spend considerably less time looking for lost belongings. Sometimes our priorities can become confused, and we can become distracted. The Bible shows us that thinking clearly and exercising self-control means living according to God's principles and surrendering to Him. It means understanding that self-control is a fruit of the Spirit (Galatians 5:23) and that we need the power of the Spirit to have real self-control.

Although as Christians our hearts are made new, our fleshly desires always fight for control. We want what we want, and we'll whine until we get it. No matter how hard we try to put a lid on our desires, they will pop up somewhere, in some way. We may trick ourselves into some semblance of self-control by saying no or cleaning up some clutter. The fruit of self-control works in us to bring into submission our behaviour as well as the impulses and emotions beneath that behaviour. Thus, more than decluttering is required. His Spirit living within begins to change our natures. We admit to the inadequacy and emptiness of trying to do it on our own. We face the reality of priorities that are out of order.

Let's not be ruled by our unbridled desires but seek to be filled with and led by the Spirit. Take Peter's wisdom in the verse above— *"Don't slip back into your old ways of living to satisfy your own desires"*—and remember: God has planned abundant blessings for you that far surpass the "stuff." Don't miss out!

Thank you, Father God, for the abundant blessings you bring into my life every day. You are my source of strength and power. I submit to you. I do not want to be ruled by unbridled desires or fall back into old, unhealthy patterns. Invade my heart once again with your truth and grace. Lead me in your path of righteousness. Amen.

Ready, Set, Run!

Day Twenty-Six
Contributed by Cathy Brown

> *But I discipline my body and bring it into subjection, lest, when I have preached to others, I myself should become disqualified.*
> —1 Corinthians 9:27, NKJV

I rounded the corner and headed into the dell, where I saw the flash of a bright-yellow oriole flitting in the dappled sunlight. *Crunch, crunch.* The pebbles under my feet sounded in easy rhythm as I took the next knoll in stride. My laboured breathing never got easier no matter how many times I ran this five-kilometre route. I felt like I was gasping for my last breath, even though I paced it with my steps: in-one-two-three-four … out-one-two-three-four-five. "Breathe deep and exhale more to avoid cramping," I told myself. During those twenty-five minutes, life was reduced to the essential elements of sucking in oxygen and working out the length and spring of each step.

I don't consider myself an athlete or runner. Real athletes thrive in that environment, increasing speed and attaining marathon status. I was thin, tall, and slightly awkward growing up. I didn't start running until I entered my first set of exams in university. It's the one thing I could do (with no car and living out of town) that helped me refresh, de-stress, and focus.

Something about pushing myself in running or weightlifting opened doors of focus and vibrancy that were *otherwise unattainable.* Yes, my body benefited, and I was healthier, but that was not the *why.* Before I understood the essentials of electrolyte replenishment, it would take me a full day to recover.

Being outside with the wind against my face was invigorating, and though it was never easy, I knew I was better for it.

Self-discipline is essential in our physical bodies and our spiritual lives. Second Peter 1:5–6 (NKJV) says: "... *giving* all diligence, *add to your faith virtue, to virtue knowledge, to knowledge self-control, to self-control perseverance* ..." (emphasis added). Peter says that if these things are ours and abound, we will not be barren nor unfruitful. Paul uses strong language when he says: "*But I discipline my body and bring it into subjection, lest, when I have preached to others, I myself should become disqualified*" (1 Corinthians 9:27, NKJV).

Although self-control (or self-discipline) is a fruit of the Spirit, it's also something God tells *us* to add to our lives. We can't use the excuse that we aren't "experts" or "naturally inclined" in this area, because God wouldn't tell us to diligently make it happen if we couldn't do it. What keeps us from abounding in self-control? Could it be a lack of intentionality, apathy, settling for less than His best, or not pushing against the resistance we feel in the process?

Self-discipline isn't just measured in whether we can fight off the temptation of devouring the entire package of jube jubes given by a kind co-worker. It's about pushing ourselves to a place that is *unattainable* except by the Spirit's power within. We cultivate the fruit of self-discipline as we persevere in the trials when it's hard even to catch our breath. We agonize in prayer, building spiritual muscle, knowing it will pay great dividends on the track. We refresh our spirits with the Water of Life. We endure, representing Him well and leaving a good example for those coming after us.

The Word challenges us not to drift with the current but to faithfully and intentionally push forward into everything that God has for us! Be encouraged today—grow stronger in the process, then look beyond the pain to the joy of finishing well.

Lord Jesus, remind me to hang in during the trials, even when it's hard to catch my breath. Help me to be constant in prayer. Refresh my spirit with your Water of Life. May I represent you well as I keep my eyes on the goal. In your holy name. Amen.

Victory over Lies

Day Twenty-Seven
Contributed by Doneka Casey

For though we walk in the world, we do not fight according to this world's rules of warfare. The weapons of the war we're fighting are not of this world but are powered by God and effective at tearing down the strongholds erected against His truth. We are demolishing arguments and ideas, every high-and-mighty philosophy that pits itself against the knowledge of the one true God. We are taking prisoners of every thought, every emotion, and subduing them into obedience to the Anointed One.
—2 Corinthians 10:3–5, VOICE

I can't pinpoint the exact time or specific circumstance when the lies began. "Being a Christian" was all I knew. I witnessed and valued many powerful moments as Jesus moved and impacted people. So what made me believe I wasn't good enough?

The busyness of church and serving often took priority, and even as a youth, I started to feel as though "being perfect" was expected of me. This expectation wasn't intentional but an innocent attempt to encourage me to do more. The problem? I saw it as a need to accomplish more and live up to my perceived expectations from others. As a natural people pleaser, it was the perfect storm. This relentless pursuit of perfection and accomplishment resulted in me pulling farther away from God and wondering what it was all for anyway. I didn't feel joy. I became consumed with church activity, attempting to show how good, dedicated, and dependable I was. I had no time for His Word, abiding or finding that personal God connection. My negative self-talk increased, and in my sorrow, my heart yearned desperately for something more—Jesus.

He heard the cry of my heart. What happened next was the beginning of something life-changing. During an unforgettable Sunday morning worship, I was overcome by emotions and a deep longing. I didn't fully understand it, but I wanted more. I longed to know my Heavenly Father intimately, and this longing intensified the mental battle. The enemy of my soul liked the deceived, busy, distracted me who was also becoming bitter and resentful. I needed the fruit of self-control to fight the battle in my mind and counterattack the onslaught of negative thoughts and lies. Satan had been launching them in full force. I felt helpless.

It was a fresh revelation that I could be victorious not by might or power, but by His Spirit who dwelled in me (Zechariah 4:6). Leaning into the Spirit's strength, I began taking every thought captive and replacing it with God's truth. I became quickly alerted to the lies and let them die before they became part of me. Self-control became submission to His truth, not just more effort and striving. My will surrendered to God brought peace of mind and a settled spirit.

I found new joy as He guided my relationships within my marriage and as a mom, daughter, sister, and friend. Leaning into His Truth, my self-control arsenal was loaded to fight back with God's authority and strength! These words from Ephesians provided me with renewed strength: *"Embrace the power of salvation's full deliverance, like a helmet to protect your thoughts from lies ..."* (Ephesians 6:18a, TPT). I was now learning the truth of 2 Corinthians to fight this battle.

Allowing the fruit of self-control to continue to mature in my life has secured my identity in Christ: *"Then you will know the truth, and the truth will set you free"* (John 8:32). I now appreciate each new victory, and I trust His continued work in me as I stay pliable and submitted.

> *Heavenly Father, thank you for exposing the lies and helping me to learn your Truth about me. You delight in me and sing for joy because of me (Zephaniah 3:17). I love abiding in your presence and listening to your heart. I know my praise defeats the enemy and ushers in your presence and peace. I choose to turn my thoughts toward your Truth daily, in Jesus' name. Amen*

No Revenge: Just Revival!

Day Twenty-Eight
Contributed by Shulammite Nasir

A [shortsighted] fool always loses his temper and displays his anger, but a wise man [uses self-control and] holds it back.
—Proverbs 29:11, AMP

Galatians 5:22–23 lists self-control as the last fruit of the Spirit. When the fruit of the Holy Spirit is growing in us, it brings changes in our character, helping us to gain strength to reject our baser whims, our unrighteous reactions, and fleshly lusts. Philippians 2:13 (CEV) says, *"God is working in you to make you willing and able to obey him."* This means submitting our thoughts, words, hearts, bodies, and actions to respond in obedience to Him. God's intention wasn't to make us weak-willed in nature, but in our fallen nature, we have come under the influence of sin. As a result, sin pushes us to satisfy legitimate wants and desires with illicit ones. Holy Spirit helps us make the right decisions through cultivating the fruit of the Spirit in our lives.

As we prioritize eternal value over the world's immediate gratification, self-control leads to perseverance (2 Peter 1:6). We experience the advantages of stewarding our lives; we gain freedom from the repeated regret of following foolish impulses. In Roman 7:21–25, Paul says that believers must maintain self-control because external and internal powers continue to attack. Like a vulnerable city, we must have defences. A wall around an ancient city was designed to keep out the enemy. Judges at the gates determined who should be allowed in and who should remain outside. Soldiers and gates enforced those decisions. Self-control is a good guard!

Paul and Silas demonstrate a picture of self-control, patience, and perseverance, even in great struggles (Acts 16). They were arrested, stripped, beaten, and thrown into the inner cell of the jail in stocks and chains simply because they were doing God's work. While in prison, they worshipped and praised God. They could have plotted their revenge or called out curses as they were being tortured, but they sang hymns and prayed. Choosing that kind of response is only attainable through the strength of the Spirit: *"About midnight, Paul and Silas were praying and singing hymns to God, and the other prisoners were listening to them"* (Acts 16:25). Their worship and praise not only helped Paul and Silas to stay strong but brought hope to those who listened. Their example of patience and self-control changed lives!

In an incredible act of discernment, Paul knew they must not run when the chains came loose and the prison doors swung open. He knew God was working something greater and something good. He didn't lose his temper because of all he had suffered, but he let God take control of the situation. Because of this, so many other lives were saved.

At times, stepping back, walking in self-control, and keeping our trust in God brings revival not just in our lives but in others' lives as well. Re-locating from Pakistan to Canada brought many more cultural changes than I could have imagined. As a young adult, I have often been ready to lose control and burst out in anger. In those times, the Holy Spirit brought me an awareness of God's promises for my life. Submission and obedience became my priority, and with the help of the Holy Spirit, I was able to control my responses and let God do His work. Turning these struggles over to Him made a difference in the unity and growth within my family.

God has a plan for you. He has anointed you from your mother's womb. Today's culture can distract you from your anointing and lead you to act as a fool who loses his temper. Be wise. Submit to God, be self-controlled, fulfill your purpose, and keep yourself from many regrets.

Father, I confess that I can't do this on my own. I choose surrender. I know it's not just about me. May lives be changed by my godly responses. Amen.

A Garden Wrestle

Day Twenty-Nine

Yet not as I will, but as you will.

—Matthew 26:39b

When I was growing up, my grandmother's living room wall displayed a modestly-framed print portraying Jesus in the garden of Gethsemane, kneeling before a big rock. His hands were folded, and His face was serene as He gazed heavenward. Above His face was a stream of light, filling the spaces in the surrounding trees with a soft and peaceful glow. The picture would readily draw one's thoughts to the journey of Jesus before the cross, but its adherence to the truth of what happened was minimal. That's simply not the way it was.

In Matthew 26:36–39, the scene is described this way:

> *Then Jesus went with his disciples to a place called Gethsemane, and he said to them, "Sit here while I go over there and pray." He took Peter and the two sons of Zebedee along with him, and he began to be sorrowful and troubled. Then he said to them, "My soul is overwhelmed with sorrow to the point of death. Stay here and keep watch with me." . . . he fell with his face to the ground and prayed, "My Father, if it is possible, may this cup be taken from me. Yet not as I will, but as you will."*

Luke, the physician, adds even more from a physical perspective: *"An angel from heaven appeared to him and strengthened him. And being in anguish, he prayed more earnestly, and his sweat was like drops of blood falling to the ground"* (Luke 22:43-44).

"Isn't there another way?" He was asking. This conversation with the Father required honesty and humility. He took His pain and questions to the Father, and He wrestled it through. He did so to align with the Father's plans and purposes, and He knew this demanded the surrender of his will.

We sense the agony of the wrestle in His heart and then the freedom of release as Jesus gives up His will to the will of his Father. Jesus reminded His disciples that He could have asked the Father, and He would have sent legions of angels to wage war and rescue Him from what was ahead. But He gave up that power to embrace a greater power (Matthew 26:53).

When Jesus left the garden, His heart was submitted. He walked into the next scene full of strength, dignity, and power, under control because He knew who was in control. Because of this submission, we see the unfolding of Christ's suffering that followed:

> *[He] suffered for you ... When they hurled their insults at him, he did not retaliate; when he suffered, he made no threats. Instead, he entrusted himself to him who judges justly.*
>
> —1 Peter 2:21–23

The Father doesn't want us to carry shame or guilt because we wrestle. It's the pathway that leads to peace, even though our circumstances may not change. We can bring him our laments and complaints, our feelings of injustice, our need for revenge, and He will listen. Spending time with Him will rein in the anxiety, anger, and loss of hope. His arms are open to embracing us in our wrestle while, at the same time, growing in us the fruit of self-control.

What does it take for us to say "as you will"? It takes a firm trust in God's plans; it takes prayer and obedience. It takes giving up our draining attempts to control and surrendering our will to His. This is a revelation that will cause us to overcome!

> *Lord Jesus, your wrestle was more intense than any I could imagine. It gives me hope and comfort to know that you understand. Help me to walk with a heart submitted to your will. In your name I pray. Amen.*

A Second Chance

Day Thirty

For the grace of God has appeared, bringing salvation for all people, training us to renounce ungodliness and worldly passions, and to live self-controlled, upright, and godly lives in the present age.

—Titus 2:11–12, ESV

If the life of Samson were a war novel or a mere story of the lives of the elite, it would rival that of anything Shakespeare wrote. Samson is a tragic hero whose astounding deeds are overshadowed by the disastrous failures in his life. He was gifted with an unparalleled physical strength to defeat the Philistines, set aside from birth for the purposes of God, but also dominated by the flesh. He had it all—but self-control.

Samson started off as a promising judge. The angel of the Lord had appeared to his infertile mother and promised her a son:

. . . you will conceive and give birth to a son . . . be careful not to drink wine or strong drink, nor eat any unclean thing . . . no razor shall come upon his head, for the boy shall be a Nazirite to God . . . and he will begin to save Israel from the hands of the Philistines."

—Judges 13:3–5, NASB

The people of Israel, who had done what was right most of the time during Joshua's time, had walked away from God, making sinful choices. They were content being slaves to the Philistines, but God, in mercy, decided to deliver them. He chose to do so with Samson. He was to live a life of dedication to God and had the mission of delivering God's people.

We know that against his parents' advice, Samson married into the enemy camp, taking a Philistine bride. Things went from bad to worse. He later slept with a prostitute, and after that, took another flawed woman named Delilah. He wanted what he wanted, and it didn't matter who got hurt. He had two choices—master his passions through God's power and obedience to His voice, or those passions would master him. None of us are capable of doing this on our own; we need God's grace and the strength of the Holy Spirit working within us.

Delilah's trickery led to his final downfall, and he was left in the end begging God to allow him one last time to use his gift of strength to fulfill his call. Samson was saying, "Work through me again. Give me a second chance to do your will." In a ruined state, without his eyes, mocked by onlookers, he found himself willing to die to avenge his enemies and realize his call. In collapsing the temple, Samson killed three thousand Philistines, more than he had defeated in his lifetime. With his numerous moral failures, lured there by deception and disobedience, his story remains heartbreaking. It's a story of life devoid of the joy of faithful obedience—one frequented by poor choices in the absence of self-control.

Like Samson, God has called us to live as set-apart ones, as holy people. At times we fail miserably, and we need to see God's redemptive work as He allows us a second chance: *"Let men... banish from their minds the very thought of doing wrong! Let them turn to... our God, for he will abundantly pardon!"* (Isaiah 55:7, TLB). Second chances reveal a God who ultimately loves His children, even when they fail. With God in control, we can *daily fulfill* our calling, bring glory to God, and cross the finish line strong.

> *Heavenly Father, you have been teaching me the joy of living a self-controlled life, where my will is submitted to the leadership of the Holy Spirit. I haven't always lived in that way. Strengthen me to stand strong in the face of deception, temptation, and my own selfish desires and plans. Thank you for your abundant pardon and the promise of a second chance. In Jesus' name. Amen.*

Small Group Helps

This devotional journey welcomes the participation of others in a small group setting, either in person or online. There are three suggested ways to read with your group.

1. A four-week group session, meeting once weekly. By having the group read one extra entry on weeks three and four, you can complete the journey in the four weeks.
2. A five-week session, reading one devotional daily but taking Sundays off.
3. A six-week session, reading five devotionals each week, taking the weekends off.

Each participant will need their own copy of the book and can journal any takeaways or questions from their daily readings. In a small group setting, all participants should be reading the devotional entries at the same time so that discussions centre around the same readings on any given week. Discussing their insights will reveal some impacting and exciting truths.

The group leader may select two to five questions from the following list for the weekly group meeting, which should run about one hour. Vary your selection of questions from the list, adapting them to your group's focus. Be sure to allow time for personal thoughts, testimonies of growth, and any questions. Keep a scriptural view as foundational, and expect God to meet with you as you gather. The preferred leadership style for this topic is facilitation, where the leader encourages both participation and time boundaries during sharing. The facilitator should be familiar with the material and keep the discussion moving.

General Discussion Questions (Choose Your Own Adventure!)

These questions are suitable for use any week.
1. Which biblical character or event was most impactful to your growth this week?
2. What life lesson did you learn from that character or event?
3. Which testimony stood out for you this week? Share what you gained from it.
4. Share one truth from this week's readings that might be relevant to pass along to a specific friend for discussion in the future.
5. Choose a scripture verse from this week's devotionals and unpack what it means in your life right now.
6. Talk about your greatest gentleness or self-control challenge right now and pray for one another.

Specific Questions Listed by Day

Day One

- Titus 3:1–2 reminds us that we must always be ready to do something helpful in a gentle and kind manner. Share with the group an opportunity you've had recently to bring the love of Jesus by doing something helpful.
- Spend some time in the New Testament reading Mark 1:40–45. What most impacts you about this story of Jesus and the leper?

Day Two

- In 1 Kings 19, we see Elijah in fear, running for his life. Why did the Lord ask him, "What are you doing here, Elijah?"?

Small Group Helps

- Has the Lord ever called you to go back to a situation so that He could use you? Share your story of encouragement with the group.

Day Three

- Share with the group a time in your life when you felt like a flickering candle, and God breathed life onto that dwindling flame in your heart.
- What are some moments in Mark's journey where you see God at work uniquely and specifically?

Day Four

- What are some things we mistakenly think about God because of our childhood events and situations?
- Is there some part of your journey where you know Jesus was stooping down to make you great? Share with your group.

Day Five

- People have often wondered what Jesus wrote on the ground as the Pharisees were waiting to stone the woman caught in adultery What are your thoughts?
- Do you ever get stirred up with second-hand offence? What has helped you to make the right choice for your heart?

Day Six

- In the Amplified version of Colossians 3:12, we're reminded that the fruit of the Spirit helps us to endure whatever unpleasantness comes, and helps us do so with a good attitude. How is this a good reminder to you in your present situation? Share with your group.

- Have you ever seen gentleness make a difference for someone who really needed it, such as a hospitalized person? Or a disabled child? Or a family member? Share your story of encouragement.

Day Seven

- Has God ever used you in the midst of someone's storm? Share your story with your group.
- It's interesting that David didn't choose to pray for Don immediately but took him back to the church for coffee first. How can you see the hand of God in how this situation played out?

Day Eight

- What do you see as the biggest change in Craig's life after he met Jesus? Share your ideas with the group.
- Is there a way that God has used the challenging parts of your life to minister to others?

Day Nine

- Proverbs 15 says that a gentle tongue is a tree of life. Who has blessed your life with their gentle and encouraging words? Give thanks to the Lord by sharing with your group.
- How do you want to model gentleness in your words toward your family and friends?

Day Ten

- Is there a Zacchaeus or a Georgie in your life who needs love and a gentle spirit? Share with your group and pray together for that person.
- What strikes you most about Georgie's story?

Small Group Helps

Day Eleven

- Jesus wants us to learn from Him how to be gentle and humble and how to find rest. Do you think you have ever chosen counterfeit gentleness? If so, share that story with your group.
- How tempting is it for you to assert control when Jesus is telling you just to submit to Him?

Day Twelve

- Jesus knew as He entered Jerusalem that Israel had rejected Him and His love for them. Describe how you would feel if your love and hugs weren't welcomed?
- We're likely all guilty of losing it with someone like Snoopy, who does crazy things they were never meant to do. How can you support those people with your love without offering approval for their foolishness?

Day Thirteen

- When Jesus washed the feet of the disciples, He took on the role of a servant or slave. How are you participating in His humility on a regular basis?
- If Jesus were to visit your group today, how much would you welcome Him to wash your feet? Is there anything that would give you hesitation? Share these thoughts with your group.

Day Fourteen

- How do you think the church universal is doing with functioning in receptivity to those who are early in their spiritual journey? Discuss.
- What made Gloria the perfect candidate to be used by the Lord in Janet's life?

Day Fifteen

- What impacted you in Brittany's story of God finding her the right husband?
- How well are we doing with making room for and appreciating other cultures in our Christian walk? How do we honour them as people created and loved by God and yet not compromise our faith?

Day Sixteen

- Can you relate to Allan's story about trying to "fix" things yourself? Explain.
- How can the church be more welcoming in practical ways for those overwhelmed in their struggle?

Day Seventeen

- How did Nehemiah demonstrate self-control when his neighbours tried to distract him?
- Are you busy swatting flies instead of staying focused on your part in building God's Kingdom? Explain.

Day Eighteen

- What was the turning point for Nicole in her challenge of change?
- What would it mean to you if you heard God tell you things would be okay "no matter what"?

Day Nineteen

- Have you ever been on the brink of disaster and about to lose control? Talk to your group about it. How did the Holy Spirit rescue you? Was it part of a learning curve, and in what way?

Small Group Helps

- What are the times and situations in your life that make you more vulnerable to stepping outside of the Spirit's control?

Day Twenty

- It cost Misty a lot to walk in the fruit of self-control. Have you ever had to pay a price for walking in obedience to the Holy Spirit? Share with your group.
- How are you encouraged by 2 Timothy 1:7?

Day Twenty-One

- We all experience Paul's struggle at times, not understanding why we do what we do, and sometimes doing what we don't want to do and hating what we decide to do. How have you experienced that struggle in your life, and how are you leaning on the Holy Spirit to help?
- What does Paul point to as the culprit in the struggle, and how do we win this fight?

Day Twenty-Two

- Consider how you might use your words to encourage someone this week by a phone call, text, or note.
- Share with your group some ways you could be using words to build up others.

Day Twenty-Three

- Abraham could have chosen simply to follow the rulebook and cut Lot out of what was rightfully his own. But he gave up his right to be right for the sake of relationship. Talk about Abraham's decision and the benefits of pursuing peaceful solutions.
- We don't always have to get our own way to solve a conflict. What does this statement mean to you?

Day Twenty-Four

- What was the importance of patience partnering with self-control in Jacob's life?
- How does the Holy Spirit help us to remain patient in delayed promises and disappointments?

Day Twenty-Five

- Peter makes it clear that self-control isn't an easy task. He reminds us not to slip back into our old ways, simply satisfying our own desires. Can you identify an area in your own life where are you have to stay on guard so that you don't slip back?
- What do you think is at the root of us needing to have our own way and needing to have more things than necessary? What can we do to pull up those unhealthy roots?

Day Twenty-Six

- What do you think Paul meant when he said that he disciplines his body so that when he preaches to others, he's not disqualified?
- How are you cultivating the fruit of self-discipline in your spiritual life?

Day Twenty-Seven

- How can we minister effectively to those who feel like they're not good enough?
- What difference did it make when the Holy Spirit showed Doneka the lies? Have you been a believer of lies, and how has God helped you to break free?

Small Group Helps

Day Twenty-Eight

- Paul and Silas laid down any need for revenge during their unjust confinement. How did their decisions affect others?
- What makes praise an effective tool in exercising self-control?

Day Twenty-Nine

- Have you ever been in a situation where you prayed, "God, isn't there another way?"? Share with your group.
- As we release our will to the will of the Father, something amazing happens. How would you describe that?

Day Thirty

- Samson had been set aside for the purposes of God, but he allowed his fleshly desires to take him off course. Is there someone you're praying for right now who has detoured off the pathway God planned for them? Share with your group and pray together for these people.
- Our God is a God of redemption and second chances. What do you think the scripture means when it says He will abundantly pardon?

Note: As a bonus, for the first eighteen months after release, contact the author at ruth.teakle@gmail.com to have one of the contributors as a guest (online only) at one of your group sessions. Details upon request.

Contributors' Biographies

Davina Boerefyn moved to Canada from India in 2004 when she married the love of her life, Timothy. As a pastor's kid, she grew up reaching the socially disadvantaged and forming mission partnerships. She is an MBA graduate with a background in finance, broadcasting, and journalism in India, Europe, and Canada. Davina actively serves her local church in various avenues of passion, as a deacon on the board and together with her husband in marriage mentoring. Davina recently opened her new Etsy shop with exceptional original photographs of iconic landmarks, scenic landscapes, cool cityscapes, and seasonal beauty. She is convinced that chocolate, coming from the cocoa plant, counts as a daily serving of vegetables!

https://explorewithdavina.etsy.com/

Cathy Brown is the mother of three adult children and blessed with an expanding family that includes the kids' amazing spouses and the grandchildren. She and her husband, Stephen, make their home in Grimsby, Ontario, where they enjoy outdoor activities like hiking, boating, and gardening. Cathy is an ordained minister with the Pentecostal Assemblies of Canada and, in the past, spent a number of years partnering with her husband in pastoral ministry. Cathy scores in the ninety-ninth percentile for anything to do with numbers! When Cathy isn't adding, subtracting, dividing, or multiplying, she's hanging out with her family or serving as Pastor of Administration at Lakemount Worship Centre, where she has been faithfully engaged in a full-time staff role for the past seventeen years.

Doneka Casey has been married to her wonderful husband, Patrick, for almost twenty-eight years. Together they've been blessed to raise an amazing son, Zachary, and in recent years welcomed their daughter-in-love, Rebekah, into their family. Doneka serves in the role of Lead Guesting Chase Producer for the longest-running daily Canadian television broadcast, *100 Huntley Street*. Along with her work commitment, Doneka makes family a priority, finding space to love them, whether near or far, connect with friends, bake some favourite treats, and enjoy a good book. Coffee is a mainstay, and Doneka is an avid walker. Doneka thoroughly enjoys worshipping at Lakemount Worship Centre in Grimsby, Ontario and cherishes her personal journey of growing more deeply in love with Jesus every day.

https://100huntley.com/

Caleb Courtney is a public secondary school computer engineering teacher. Caleb is also a well-known worship leader, musician, and ordained minister with the Pentecostal Assemblies of Canada. He researches and writes on the history of Pentecostalism in Canada and is the co-author of a book titled *Canadian Pentecostal Reader: The First Generation of Pentecostal Voices in Canada, 1907–1925* (CPT Press, 2021). Caleb plays French horn for the International Symphony Orchestra, a cross-border collaboration between musicians in Michigan and Ontario. Caleb enjoys life together with his wife, Stephanie, and their four kids in Sarnia, Ontario.

Contributors' Biographies

Misty Duggan lives in St. Catharines, Ontario with her husband, Jamie, of twenty-three years. She's mother to their four children: Kayleigh, Kaleb, Judie, and Lucas. She's an animal lover, enjoying a dog, cat, and parrot in their home. She and her family recently lived in East Africa for four years, where she helped children in need through education, nutrition, health care, and shelter. She is currently the Finance and Administration Manager at Grimsby Benevolent Fund Community Services, a local non-profit organization that assists individuals and households in meeting their basic needs. She faithfully attends Lakemount Worship Centre in Grimsby, Ontario, where she serves in children's ministries.

https://gbfgrimsby.com/

Craig Forbes has been serving the Lord since 1966. Following thirty years as a professional bus driver in the city of Toronto, Craig retired with ministry in his heart. He was ordained as a minister of the gospel in December 2022, and in February 2023 began a position with Lakemount Worship Centre as their evangelism pastor. He believes that his best years are ahead of him and is passionate and honoured to serve the Lord and walk in His calling. Although Craig may often be found on a charity ride with other bikers or visiting the migrant workers at a nearby farm, he is best known for cooking up a massive batch of his amazing jerk chicken. Craig is a father of four and grandfather of six. He and his wife, Stacey, and their dogs, Deogi (an Airedale terrier) and Sage (a French bulldog), reside in Stoney Creek, Ontario.

Allan Gallant was born in Cape Breton, Nova Scotia. He and his wife, Bonnie, have five grown children and eight wonderful grandchildren. Together he and Bonnie founded Agora Network Ministries in 2019, a ministry that provides mental health seminars, presentations, and resources to the faith community. Allan's story of his journey through a serious health crisis, PTSD, anxiety, and depression, and his road to restoration, are chronicled in his book, *The Beautiful Strokes of God*. Allan loves to ride his motorbike and equally loves the Toronto Maples Leafs and the Toronto Blue Jays. Bonnie and Allan reside in Thorold, Ontario and attend Northend Church in St. Catharines, Ontario.

https://agoranetworkministries.com/

Brittany Jeyaseelan and her husband, Kenneth, are currently based in Ontario, Canada. Starting their married life in a country neither of them were born in, they have embraced their multinational life and are thankful for the opportunity to minister in the United States, Canada, India, and beyond. Brittany's career skills are presently focused in the areas of marketing and web development management. More importantly, Brittany presently hosts and leads a mentorship and Bible study breakfast life group for ladies, and she serves on the Rapha Healing Prayer team. She is passionate about serving in her local church and being a part of Kingdom advancement around the world.

Kathy Mullen is a retired occupational therapist. She is a wife, mother of two, and grandmother of two. Kathy speaks internationally with her husband, Dr. Grant Mullen, about how God wants to heal our hearts and transform the way we think. Her special interest is in forgiveness as a gateway to healing. She's also involved with small groups, is a church elder, an inner healing prayer minister, and a worship artist with fabric. Kathy is the co-author of *Emotionally Free* and over twenty teaching DVDs. You can see her ministry at drgrantmullen.com and her worship art at liftedup.ca.

Contributors' Biographies

Shulammite Nasir is a very passionate young adult with a huge heart for missions all around the world. She carries the burden for young adults and raising up leaders from the next generation. Shulammite helps to coordinate and direct Alpha at Church of Pentecost Pakistan and is working with organizations like Wycliffe Bible Institute for Bible translation in different languages. She's also working with missions and leadership in additional countries. She's a second-year intern at Lakemount Worship Centre, where she serves with dedication and commitment. Her heart is to spread the gospel to unreached nations and build the Kingdom of God through raising up passionate, Christ-loving leaders who walk in integrity, vision, and faith.

https://www.coppakistan.org/
https://alphacanada.org/

David Pitcher was born in St. John's, Newfoundland. The eldest son of Salvation Army officer parents, he had the privilege of getting to know much of Canada as a child, as the family ministered across the map from Newfoundland to British Columbia. He accepted the gift of God's love and the news of salvation at the age of four. He and his wife of over fifty years, Donna, were married in St. Catharines, Ontario, and as Salvation Army officers, they too have served in several appointments throughout Ontario, Manitoba, and British Columbia. They've had the joy of parenting their three children and love to celebrate and cheer on the grandchildren. Since retirement from active Salvation Army Officer service, they've lived and volunteered in ministry in the Niagara Region. David has always found strength and assurance in God's Word, a favourite verse being Proverbs 3:6: *"In all thy ways acknowledge Him, and He will direct thy paths"* (KJV).

Sunita Ramadeen was born and raised in Georgetown, Guyana and migrated to Canada in 1989. She is mother to five children—biological twins and three adopted children. She owns a ladies' dress shop and is a fashion consultant and personal shopper. She loves to travel, especially if it includes time to shop at designer outlets. She has been happily married to her amazing husband, Paul, for almost thirty-one years.

Sunita serves on the Rapha and Prayer teams at Lakemount Worship Centre and has just completed the Year One Ministry Internship. She serves the Lord with passion and grace and has a heart to see the broken find their identity in Christ.

Before emigrating to Canada, Mark Soppitt spent five years as a police officer and seven years as a pastor in the UK, where he was born and raised. In 2005, in response to a call to pastor a church in Niagara Falls, Mark, his wife, Janet, and their five children arrived in Canada.

In 2008, Mark entered a very dark and difficult season of depression and had to step down from his role as pastor in 2012. Mark's restoration has included work in manufacturing, sales, and personal care. He is currently writing worship songs and pursuing study to become a biblical counsellor. He enjoys exercise, long walks with his wife, movies, and music. He serves his home church in trauma healing, worship, and prayer ministries.

Nicole Warden was born in Quebec and, after some time in northern Ontario, moved to St. Catharines, where she met and married Bob, her husband of over forty-five years. Her career path has embodied various areas of accounting and personnel management. She has served locally and regionally in altar prayer ministry, women's prayer initiatives, women's ministry and youth conference intercessory teams, and building prayer ministry in the local church. She delights in seeing Holy Spirit bring healing and freedom to individuals through the power of prayer. Nicole presently serves on staff as Prayer Pastor at her local church.

About the Author

Ruth Teakle lives with her husband, Carl, in Grimsby, Ontario. She loves to spend time with her three children and their spouses and her eleven grandchildren. Although retired, Ruth serves as a support staff member at Lakemount Worship Centre in Grimsby, Ontario, where she previously served on full-time and part-time staff for over twenty years. Her roles varied from overseeing small groups and missions to prayer and pastoral care. As well she has led and assisted with numerous short-term missions to the Caribbean, Eastern Europe, Ukraine, South America, northern Ontario, and Quebec.

On the home front, Ruth and Carl have fostered over 130 children during a twenty-five-year period. Ruth has worked within the Correctional Services of Canada, volunteered with numerous summer camp programs through both Girls Guides of Canada and the Salvation Army, directed an annual city-wide Christmas toy program, and filmed a national training course for telephone prayer partners. She also served for many years in local, area, and national capacities with Aglow International Canada prior to pastoral ministry.

Ruth's academic pursuits have included studies at Lakeshore Teachers' College, Brock University (Bachelor of Arts), and Wagner University (Master of Practical Ministries). She has completed ESL studies, and is a Certified Anger Management Specialist and Trauma Healing Master Facilitator. Prior to taking additional Religious Studies courses with Global University in preparation for ordained ministry, Ruth enjoyed a successful thirty-two-year career as an elementary school teacher.

Ruth is an ordained minister with the Pentecostal Assemblies of Canada, with a heart to see people become passionate followers of Christ. She also has a strong sense of mission to help disciple them into healthy connections with God and others. Her challenging but victorious personal journey makes her well-qualified to share on the importance of cultivating gentleness and self-control as we walk in the power and fruit of the Holy Spirit.

Additional Note: Ruth's first devotional, *Changing Seasons*, is a pocket/purse-sized devotional full of encouragement from God's Word written especially for seniors, and it's one of the GODQUEST SERIES available only through The Bible League, Canada. bibleleague.ca/resources/godquest/.

Pursuing Patience, Pursuing Peace, Choosing Love, Choosing Kindness, Cultivating Faith, and *Experiencing Joy* are available through Word Alive Press and numerous national and international outlets.

Ruth has also authored a delightfully illustrated children's book for children ages four to nine, *Joshua Wonders: What Does the Tooth Fairy Do with My Teeth?* available through numerous national and international outlets.